The
LOST
PYRAMID

M. Zakaria Goneim, M.A.

CHIEF INSPECTOR OF ANTIQUITIES, SAKKARA, EGYPT

The
LOST
PYRAMID

RINEHART & COMPANY, INC., New York

Grateful acknowledgment is made to the Department of Antiquities of the Egyptian Government, Cairo, for permission to use the illustrations in this book.

INTRODUCTION

BY M. ZAKARIA GONEIM

THIS IS THE STORY OF MY DISCOVERY, AT SAKKARA, NEAR Cairo, of a hitherto unknown pyramid of the Third Egyptian Dynasty (2780–2720 B.C.). It is not the full story; that will take many years to write, for the area to be excavated is so enormous that at least ten years' work lies ahead. Nor does it pretend to be the final, definitive work on the excavations in a form suitable for my fellow archaeologists, though I hope that they, too, will find it of some value. Such a work, with plans and drawings and a detailed description of all the finds down to the last pot-sherd, will eventually be published by the Department of Antiquities of the Egyptian Government, under whose auspices the work is being carried out.

However, such a heartening interest has been shown in the discovery by the press of the world, by newspapers, magazines, and radio organizations, that I have been encouraged to attempt this shorter work for the general reader. The facts which I have given are as accurate as I can hope to make them, bearing in mind that the book has been written within a few months of the clearance of the sarcophagus chamber, or, as I prefer to call it, the

Introduction

"Dummy Burial" beneath the unfinished pyramid. At the same time, it must also be borne in mind that in work of this kind new discoveries sometimes call for a revision of earlier theories, and it may be that in subsequent volumes modifications of my present beliefs may have to be made in the light of later excavations.

This book also contains a considerable amount of information relating to pyramid building which will already be familiar to trained archaeologists. I make no apology for including this, since I have tried to make the book understandable to the many millions who come fresh to the study of Egyptology. A grounding, however brief, in early Egyptian history, in Ancient Egyptian customs, building methods, etc., is essential for an intelligent understanding of this new discovery. I have also tried, as best I can, to sketch in the background of the work, to enable readers to share in the day-to-day labor of excavation, with its trials and setbacks, its "detective work," its moments of disappointment as well as of glory.

For helping me to paint this picture I must thank especially Mr. Leonard Cottrell, who shares with me a deep interest in Egyptology, and whose books and radio broadcasts have done much to stimulate interest in the subject among non-specialists. I have enjoyed Mr. Cottrell's friendship for a number of years; he has been present with me at Sakkara on several occasions, and when this book was proposed, he kindly agreed to assist in the preparation of the text.

I am especially grateful to the Prime Minister of

Introduction

Egypt, Gamal Abdl Nasser, for the kindness and encouragement he has shown to me and to other Egyptian archaeologists; also, of course, to the Department of Antiquities of the Egyptian Government, which made it possible for me to work at Sakkara, and which financed the excavations. My particular thanks are due to the Minister of Education, Lieutenant-Colonel Kamal El Din Hussein, and the Director of the Department, Dr. Mustapha Amer, without whose encouragement and support the work could not have continued.

Among the many distinguished scholars who have helped me I would like to mention Dr. William C. Hayes, Curator of the Egyptian Department of the Metropolitan Museum of Art, New York; Professor Walter B. Emery, of University College, London, England, whose work on the First and Second Dynasty tombs at Sakkara is well-known; Mr. I. E. S. Edwards, of the British Museum, who kindly read the manuscript; Professor Hermann Kees, the distinguished Egyptologist; Madame C. H. Desroche Noblecourt of the Louvre Museum; Dr. Hanns Stock, of the University of Munich; and Monsieur Jean-Phillippe Lauer, Architect at Sakkara for the Department of Antiquities, who has spent a lifetime in the study and restoration of the famous Step Pyramid of Djoser, near which the newly discovered monument was found.

M. Zakaria Goneim

FOREWORD

BY LEONARD COTTRELL

WHEN AN AMATEUR OF ARCHAEOLOGY ATTEMPTS TO write a book on that subject, it is not uncommon for the author to ask a specialist to write a preface to his work; but it is a different matter when a professional archaeologist invites an amateur to furnish such an introduction. When Mr. Goneim kindly asked me to do this, I accepted only on condition that I should not be expected to assess the technical accuracy of the book—that is outside my competence—but to confine myself to an appreciation of the man and his work. Also, there may be some justification for such a preface, since I have a slight personal responsibility for the appearance of this book.

Mr. Goneim is a scholar and a professional Egyptologist, and in due course he will publish the results of his excavations under the auspices of the Egyptian Department of Antiquities in a detailed, scientific form suitable for other scholars. But that will take some time. Meanwhile I believe that there exists, outside the study and the lecture room, a widespread audience for a book on the discovery of the "new" pyramid which, while being scholarly and accurate, would be written mainly for the general reader. Mr. Goneim was already thinking along these lines when I made the suggestion to him. He has, I believe, what is not always found among specialists—a burning passion for his chosen subject and a gift for communicating it in simple terms. I was therefore delighted when he agreed to write such a work, and this is the result.

Of all the antiquities of Ancient Egypt, the pyramids probably hold pride of place in most people's minds, as is proved by the numerous books written on the subject, and the world-wide interest which was aroused when Mr. Goneim discovered, at Sakkara, a hitherto unknown pyramid of the Third Egyptian Dynasty (*circa* 2780 B.C.). The excavations have as yet hardly begun, and it may well be that ten or more years may have to elapse before the final results are made known. This may surprise people who imagine that archaeological excavation consists largely in digging a big hole in the ground. The monument which Mr. Goneim has discovered measures approximately 400 feet by 400 feet, and in addition is surrounded by subsidiary buildings enclosed by a wall measuring approximately 1,800 feet by about 650 feet. If one may judge by the substructure of Djoser's Pyramid, built approximately during the same period, the rock beneath will almost certainly contain many long subterranean galleries leading to store chambers and perhaps the burial chambers of the king and his family. Remains of other buildings may be discovered within the outer enclosure, which may also cover other galleries and burial chambers. The magnitude of the task which Mr. Goneim and his staff face during the coming years is obvious. This is, indeed, one of the most exciting archaeological discoveries made in Egypt since the discovery of the tomb of Tutankhamen in 1922.

What manner of man is the discoverer?

Mohammed Zakaria Goneim belongs to the new generation of Egyptian archaeologists. During the past half century most of the great Egyptologists have been Europeans or Americans. One remembers such names as Maspéro (French); Borchardt (German); Reisner, Winlock, Nelson (American); Petrie, Carter, Peet, Brunton (British); Naville, Jéquier (Swiss) —to name only a handful. In the Antiquities Service itself most of the important posts used to be held by Europeans, since until comparatively recent times there was no trained cadre of Egyptian-born archaeologists. However, during the past thirty years a considerable number of Egyptians have studied Egyptian archaeology, mainly at Cairo University, under European professors, and today all the principal posts in the Antiquities Service of the Egyptian Government are held by Egyptians. Mr. Goneim is one of them.

He studied Egyptology at Cairo University, under such men as Percy Newberry and Herman Junker. His first post in the Antiquities Service was as Assistant Archaeologist at Sakkara, the place to which he has recently returned as Keeper of the Necropolis and Chief Inspector. During the intervening period, he has been successively Inspector of Antiquities at Assuan, Inspector at Sohag, then at Edfu; after which he was appointed Keeper of the Theban Necropolis at Luxor. From this he was promoted to Chief Inspector of Antiquities for Upper Egypt, during which time he carried out important excavations at Luxor and in the Theban temples. In 1951 he was made Keeper of the Necropolis at Sakkara and Chief Inspector for this very important area, where, incidentally, he first began his career as an archaeologist fourteen years before.

I first met Zakaria Goneim in 1947, when he was Chief Inspector for Upper Egypt and stationed at Luxor. At that time my knowledge of Ancient Egypt was of a most superficial kind, though the subject had attracted me since childhood. From our first meeting I recognized in Goneim a man who not only knew his subject but had a passionate love for it. In spite of his many duties, he found time to take me personally to the Theban Necropolis, including the Valley of the Kings, and to answer patiently my many questions, reawakening my dormant interest so that from that moment onward I became a devotee of Ancient Egypt. In fact, my various publications on this and kindred subjects owe their origin directly to those conversations with Zakaria Goneim in his house at Luxor seven years ago.

This patient willingness to explain was, I discovered, a personal characteristic of Goneim, and was readily extended to anyone who was genuinely interested in Ancient Egypt. He was always approachable and always kind. I have since met many visitors to Egypt who owe their first introduction to Egyptology to the young Chief Inspector at Luxor. Zakaria once said to me: "I divide mankind into two classes—those who are interested in antiquity and those who aren't. And this division cuts across all races, nations, and social groups. There are some who love the Necropolis. They may be poor people, not learned, not even articulate, but they *want* to learn. There are others, some of them quite distinguished people, some of them quite charming people, but they are not really interested. . . ."

That observation is typical of the man.

In appearance Goneim is short, dark, thickset, with a high, domed forehead. Most of the time he wears dark glasses as a protection against the fierce Egyptian sun in which he normally works. When he removes them, his eyes twinkle with fun and good humor. In fact, he is the very opposite of the conventional conception of the archaeologist. He is no dour, scholarly pedant, but a man who loves life and people. To him, as he once said to me, "the ancient Egyptians are not dead but living." His interest is not in the dry bones of the past but in reclothing them with living flesh. Often, in the middle of a serious and learned discussion on some fine point of scholarship, he will break into chortles of laughter as he recalls some amusing incident connected with his work, or tells a story, usually against himself. By altering one word one could apply to Zakaria Goneim the remark which a Scottish divine once addressed to Dr. Samuel Johnson: "I, too, wished to be an archaeologist,[1] but cheerfulness would keep breaking in. . . ."

Nevertheless, Goneim *is* an archaeologist, and a good

---

[1] In the original version "a philosopher."

one. The story he tells within these pages is one of careful, patient research and endeavor, in which there are no wild theories, no seeking after sensation. Those who follow in his footsteps can be sure that they will always remain on firm ground.

Scholars will admire the skill and economy with which the work has been carried out. By a series of bold and masterly calculations, Goneim has produced one of the most accurately placed and economically executed of archaeological digs. His patience, persistence, and acumen have leaped the gap of fifteen dynasties.

The general reader will find another satisfaction. As he follows the discoverer in his search for the pyramid, stands at his side when he penetrates the great entrance gallery, and shares his excitement as he breaks through the sealed blocking wall which leads to the sarcophagus chamber, the reader will find passages in which the humanity, imagination and enthusiasm of the excavator breaks through the hard crust of scholarship. He also will experience the awe and wonder of penetrating for the first time into galleries and chambers which have not known a human footstep since 2700 B.C.—a period when nine tenths of the recorded history of mankind had yet to be written.

Highgate, London.   Leonard Cottrell
March, 1956

CONTENTS

The
LOST
PYRAMID

ONE

The Father of Pyramids

I AM ASSUMING THAT MANY READERS OF THIS BOOK WILL
not be familiar with the detailed history of Ancient Egypt.
I hope, therefore, that those who have such knowledge
will forgive a short introduction to the early Egyptian
dynasties in order that the many who are new to the subject may be able to put the recent discoveries into their
proper perspective.

The Nile Valley is now generally accepted as the
home of the earliest civilization on this planet. When the
glacial period ended in Europe and the rains decreased,
there was a convergence of the nomadic peoples of North
Africa upon the Nile Valley, attracted by the abundant
and perennial supply of water. In early Neolithic times,
probably as long ago as 6000–5000 B.C., these people,
who were of mixed races, combining elements from the
west and east as well as from the south, and who were
originally nomadic hunters, began to settle in the Valley,
where the annual flooding of the Nile, bearing its life-
giving fertile mud, provided the means for living per-
manently in one place. Over an immense stretch of time
the primitive Egyptians learned to control their river,

or at least to predict its probable behavior. They learned to keep records of the water level at certain seasons over a long period of time, and from these were able to predict with accuracy the degree of flooding. They had to keep records, and this may have been one of the main reasons for the invention of writing. But every year many landmarks were obliterated, and this brought about the development of a precise system of surveying, so that the land could be accurately parceled out; this in turn may have led to the development of geometry, which was later applied to the construction of buildings.

So civilization grew up, although for a very long period the Egyptians were not a united people, but lived in separate cantonments scattered along the huge, winding river, each governed by its local chieftain. Throughout this period the independent tribes fought one with the other, and sometimes one powerful lord would subdue several of his neighbors, or several petty kingdoms would federate for aggression or defense. So gradually the units of government would grow larger, until a time came when Egypt was divided into two kingdoms, one of Upper Egypt and the other of Lower Egypt. Finally the king of Upper Egypt conquered the north and founded a unified kingdom.[1] This was Narmer, named also Menes, and he was the founder of what historians call the First Dynasty, which began in approximately 3200 B.C.

---

[1] Nevertheless the memory of this archaic division of Egypt into Upper and Lower Kingdoms persisted long after the whole country had become one. One of the titles of the Pharaohs was "King of Upper and Lower Egypt."

Incidentally these dynasties, as we call them, are not necessarily strictly accurate. They were first set down by a fourth century, B.C., Egyptian historian named Manetho, who wrote a history of Egypt, in the Greek language. Manetho divided the names of the Pharaohs, which he knew from the ancient records, into thirty royal houses, but not all his divisions are correct. Nevertheless, modern historians continue to use Manetho's list for convenience. A list of dynasties is given at the end of this book (pp. 169–71).

The period which I have described, that of petty wars preceding the unification of Egypt, was of long duration, and antedated by more than a thousand years the historical Egypt which we know from written records. For instance, to the Pharaoh Tutankhamen, who reigned some fourteen centuries before Christ, Menes was as distant as Nero is from us. Nevertheless, from the graves of this remote period six thousand years ago, we know that Egyptian civilization was already well developed, the calendric system was known and instituted, writing was known, and the arts of pottery, jewelry, gold work, weapon-making, etc., had reached a high level of achievement. We call this epoch before the beginnings of written history the Pre-Dynastic Period. The stretch of time which immediately followed it, that of the first two dynasties, historians call the Archaic Period (3200–2780 B.C.), a time of consolidation and development of the united kingdom. With the accession of Djoser, the first king of the Third Dynasty (2780 B.C.), the Old Kingdom begins, the period of the pyramid builders with which this book will mainly deal.

The original capital of Menes, or Narmer, was at This, in Upper Egypt, but in his campaigns against the Lower Kingdom he used as a base the city of Memphis, which stood about ten miles south of what is now Cairo. After the beginning of the Third Dynasty his successors ruled the consolidated Egyptian kingdom from Memphis itself, and until the very end of the Old Kingdom (2258–17 B.C.) Memphis remained the capital. It was the home of such mighty monarchs as Khufu, who built the Great Pyramid; of Chephren, his successor, builder of the Second Pyramid; of Menkaure, and many others. The city itself lay near the river, where a few relics still remain. The chief necropolis or burial place of the kings and their nobles was on the desert plateau to the west, which is called Sakkara.[2]

In Chapter Two I shall describe the kings of the Third Dynasty, one of whom, Sekhem-Khet ("Powerful of Body"), appears to have built the pyramid which I have recently discovered. But in this chapter I intend only to paint a general picture of the Necropolis of Sakkara itself, so that readers may more readily understand the geographical site of the discovery, and to describe the Step Pyramid of Nether-er-Inhet—also named Nether-er-Khet and Djoser—the first king of the Third Dynasty.

---

[2] The name probably derives from the god Ptah-Soker-Osiris, patron of this necropolis.

The Father of Pyramids

To anyone who has a feeling for the remote past, Sakkara is surely one of the most fascinating places in Egypt; and it is a pity that many of the thousands of visitors who yearly visit the Giza pyramids never make the additional journey of a few miles southward to see the much greater necropolis of the Memphite kings. Let us imagine, then, that having admired the Great Pyramid of Khufu and its neighbors, you have turned off the main road and taken the lesser road to Sakkara, skirting the high desert plateau which accompanies you on your right.

As your car bumps its way along the narrow road, you pass groups of men working in the fields. Here a man guides a plough behind two yoked oxen; another, in long robe and white turban, bends over a primitive pump used for raising the water from one canal to another. You are looking at things which have changed hardly at all since the days of the pyramid builders; in fact, you can still see in tombs of that period reliefs and paintings showing similar scenes. The flat green valley of the Nile stretches away to your left, blotched with the deeper green of palms, and on the far horizon rise the desert cliffs on the eastern bank, from which the ancient builders quarried the stone for the casing of the pyramids.

Now turn your eyes in the other direction, toward the desert plateau a few hundred yards away to your right. Soon a group of pyramids looms up, the Abusir group, built by four kings of the Fifth Dynasty—Sahure, Nieuserre, Neferir-kare, and Nefer-ef-re—and almost before they have

7

dropped behind you see the Step Pyramid of Djoser rising magnificently above the edge of the plateau, some miles to the south. That is at Sakkara, and if you look even closer you will see a small white speck on the very edge of the plateau, my house where I live and work.

As the car turns right to cross the valley, Djoser's Step Pyramid is straight ahead of you, but leftward still more pyramids appear, rising giant-like out of the haze, the mighty monuments of Snofru at Dashur, one of which is almost as large as that of Khufu itself. Suddenly you have left behind the cultivated land and the car's wheels spin in the soft sand. As you swing up the curving track you see deep hollows and high mounds of broken potsherds, the debris of a century of excavation. For the Necropolis of Sakkara is one of the most widely dug sites in the whole of Egypt.

You get out of the car; your feet crunch in rubble, and a cool wind blows across the acres of billowing golden sand. Beyond, to the west, lies the western desert, as sterile and empty as it was in the days of the Pharaohs. But immediately ahead of you rises the huge Step Pyramid of Djoser, first king of the Third Dynasty (2800 B.C.) —the oldest large stone structure in the world.

Though Djoser's monument dominates Sakkara, there are several other royal tombs in the area which are even earlier. The oldest are the large mastabas—tombs of the First Dynasty, recently excavated by Professor Walter B. Emery, to the north of Sakkara. These are huge rectangular structures of mud-brick, each with a central burial chamber surrounded by many smaller rooms which were intended to contain provisions for the after-life. At this period, the Ancient Egyptians seem to have believed that the life after death would be lived in or near the tomb itself, which appears to have been made in imitation of the king's palace. Even the slaves and household servants of the dead monarch seem to have accompanied him to death, since around some of the tombs Emery found a large number of small cells each containing human bones. This barbarous custom, a relic of the days before the Egyptians became civilized, seems to have been abandoned shortly after this period, the place of the servants being taken by small statuettes, called ushabtis ("answerers"), which, by a process of sympathetic magic, were endowed with the powers of real servants.

Several First Dynasty tombs have so far been unearthed at Sakkara, bearing the names of the kings Hor-aha, Zer, Vadji, Vdemu and Ka-a of Djet. Many years ago Sir Flinders Petrie discovered tombs bearing these kings' names at Abydos, in Upper Egypt, and it is not yet known whether the kings were actually buried at Abydos or Sakkara. However, it was a common practice at that time for a king to have two tombs, a northern and a southern tomb, representing him in his dual capacity as ruler of Upper and Lower Egypt. And Professor Emery believes that the kings of the First Dynasty were actually buried at Sakkara, the Abydos monuments being only cenotaphs of these kings.

These tombs had been plundered in antiquity, like

most Egyptian sepulchers, although stone jars and other funerary remains were found, as well as fragments of gold leaf which may have covered the walls of the central chamber. The mud-brick walls also showed evidence of having been subjected to intense heat, suggesting that at some time the contents had been set alight, either by enemies of the dead kings or by later intruders who wished to drive away the spirits of the dead in order to make use of the tombs for their own burials. This was a common practice in ancient Egypt.

Next in chronological order come the tombs of the Second Dynasty, situated to the southwest of Djoser's pyramid enclosure. Of these only the substructures remain, the upper parts having been destroyed, probably by King Unis when he built his mortuary temple. Clay sealings found in the subterranean galleries bear the names of two Second Dynasty kings, Ni-nether and Ra-neb, but nothing remains of their bodies or funerary equipment. Instead, the galleries have been filled at a much later date by hundreds of mummies, most of which have still to be removed. In the three thousand years during which the necropolis was in constant use, the plundered tombs of the long dead were often used by later intruders.

Up to the beginning of the Third Dynasty the Ancient Egyptians built in mud-brick, though sometimes the central chamber was lined with stone, e.g., that of Khy Khasekhem ui at Abydos. Then came one of those revolutionary changes which occur from time to time in the history of man's development, changes which a few short years enable him to transform his environment and vastly increase his powers. Such landmarks in civilization were, for example, the invention of the wheel and the steam engine. In this case it was the invention of building in stone.

Traditionally the man responsible for this great step forward was Imhotep, Chief Architect of King Djoser, who is generally regarded as the first king of the Third Dynasty.[3] At this time the consolidation of the Upper and Lower Kingdoms under unified rule was complete, and the kings ruled from Memphis. Imhotep was revered by later generations of Egyptians as a god, and the scribes would pour out a libation to him before beginning their work. Many of his alleged sayings were memorized, and when the Greeks came to Egypt they identified Imhotep with Æsculapius, their god of medicine.

Certainly he must have been a man of titanic genius, and his step pyramid, the world's first large monument made of stone, stirs the sensitive imagination even more than the later and better-known pyramids of Khufu and Khafre.

Here you may see the very beginning of architecture, the first attempt by man to build monumentally in stone. Even today, after generations of plunderers have stripped its finely masoned limestone casing and blurred the clean sharp edges of its steps, Djoser's great monument still stirs the heart; not only the pyramid itself but the marvelous

---

[3] Though there is no definite proof of this; the Papyras Westear mentions Neb-ka as the first king.

complex of courts and buildings which once surrounded it.[4]

Because the new pyramid which I have discovered belongs to the same type as that of Djoser, and, indeed, may have been built by one of that king's family, I shall devote the rest of this chapter to an explanation of how this type of monument came to be invented and the purpose which it served.

From the earliest times the Ancient Egyptians paid great attention to the welfare of their dead in the afterlife. We have all heard of the Egyptian custom of mummification, but long before they learned the art of embalming their dead, the bodies of the great were buried with extreme care, and were surrounded by furniture, ornaments, weapons, food, and other objects which it was believed would be required in the life beyond the grave.

So the Egyptian religion was not only for the living but for the dead. Man was believed to live after death in much the same way in which he had lived on earth. To ensure this it was essential to preserve the body from corruption. Also the deceased had to be aware of the ritual which must be observed when addressing the gods and spirits in the Underworld. It was these conditions which gave rise to funerary architecture—structures which would ensure the preservation of the body and its funerary equipment both from the climatic denudation and from robbery. Accordingly the burial chamber was excavated deeper and

---

[4] Leonard Cottrell, *The Lost Pharaohs*; London, 1950.

deeper underground, and cunning devices were developed to block its entrance and passageways. Also, to enable relatives and funerary priests to perform the funerary cult, a place was reserved for offerings, as near as possible to the *stele* or false door which would enable the *ka* or double of the dead to partake of these offerings.

I have mentioned the huge mud-brick tombs of the First Dynasty kings in which there was a large central chamber surrounded by smaller rooms. Later this type of tomb gave way to another in which the burial chamber and surrounding rooms were cut out of the rock and approached by a deep shaft. The part of the tomb above ground consisted of a rectangular structure, usually of mud-brick but later of stone masonry, in which there was a small, walled-in chamber called the *serdab*, containing a statue of the dead man, called the ka statue. The Ancient Egyptians seem to have believed that the ka of the dead, recognizing its statue—which was lifelike—would be able to inhabit it and to receive the food offerings which were presented outside the tomb or in an adjoining room; a "false door" was provided through which the spirit could pass to receive the offerings.

We call these tombs *mastabas*, an Arabic word meaning "bench," because they resemble the dried-mud benches which one often sees outside the homes of the Egyptian peasants.

The Step Pyramid of Djoser began life as a simple stone mastaba. There were five stages in its development. First the king's architect built a large mastaba, not unlike

a similar tomb built for Djoser at Bet Khallaf, in Upper
Egypt, but whereas the latter was oblong and built of
mud-bricks, the mastaba at Sakkara was square and built of
stone blocks. During the King's reign the structure was
extended on all four sides, but as the extension was on a
lower level a step was formed.[5]

Again the architect altered the plan, making it oblong,
but still apparently he or his master was not satisfied. For
a fourth time he enlarged the structure, and then did
something which no tomb builder had ever done before.
On top of the original large, flat mastaba he built a series
of three others, each smaller than the one below. Thus was
created the first step pyramid, the father of all the pyramids of Egypt. Evidently delighted with this, the king
decided to make it even bigger. He enlarged the base still
more until it measured 411 by 385 feet. And on top of
this he built his final monument, six superimposed terraces,
encased with fine limestone quarried from the Tura and
Masura hills, on the opposite side of the river. This building, without the limestone casing which was removed in
later times, is the structure which we see today. It should
be noted that the building is of rectangular plan, not
square, as was the case with later pyramids.

But the pyramid was only the central feature of a
huge complex of stone buildings. In earlier times the
tombs of the kings were usually surrounded by a wall,
within which offerings were made to the spirit of the dead

---

[5] It is important to remember that these tombs were built *during the
lifetime* of their owners, not afterward.

monarch. But Imhotep went much further than this. He surrounded his step pyramid with an enormous wall enclosing an area of about 35 acres (909 by 1,785 feet), a hundred times bigger than the area of the great brick tomb of Nagada, long attributed to Menes. Inside this enclosure he built a number of stone buildings, also encased in fine limestone masonry, the like of which is unknown anywhere else in Egypt. It seems that some were connected with what is called the "Sed Festival," which was of very ancient origin. In very early times the ancient kings were probably put to death after having reigned for a certain number of years. This is in accordance with similar customs still found among primitive tribes. Upon the vigor of the king depended the fertility of the land, the prosperity of Egypt, and the welfare of the people over whom he ruled. When his powers began to fail with increasing years, the monarch was ceremonially slain and a new king took his place. This may have occurred after he had occupied the throne for thirty years.

With the growth of civilization, this custom was abandoned in favor of a religio-magical ceremony in which the kingship was ritually renewed. Little is known concerning the details of this ceremony, but part of it seems to have consisted of an offering to the gods of the Upper and Lower Kingdoms, after which the king was recrowned. There is also a curious relief on the walls of one of the subterranean galleries below the pyramid enclosure which shows King Djoser, wearing the Double Crown, in a running posture. It has been suggested that part of the ceremonial may have included a ritual sprint performed by the king to test his vitality. I shall have more to say about this ceremony in later chapters.

The interesting feature of the buildings surrounding the enclosure of this step pyramid is that they appear to be *dummy* buildings for use by the king in connection with his welfare in the after-life. Possibly, therefore, the Ancient Egyptians believed that this necessity for periodical renewal and rededication would occur even after the king had died—a never-ending cycle of death and rebirth.

However, although many theories have been advanced to explain the purpose of this jubilee festival, the available facts are meager, and the same applies to Egyptian funerary customs in this remote period—the very dawn of Egyptian dynastic history. There is, for instance, the curious fact that several kings of this early period built more than one tomb. Djoser built, in addition to his Step Pyramid, a large mastaba at Bet Khallaf. Aha built a tomb at Abydos, but there is another large mastaba bearing his name at Sakkara. Snofru, the first king of the Fourth Dynasty, completed at Medum a pyramid perhaps begun by his predecessor Huni; but there are two huge pyramids at Dashur which also bear his name. Other examples could be quoted. In fact, the whole history of this remote epoch abounds in unsolved mysteries. Far less is known about it than, for example, the Eighteenth Dynasty, the time of Tutankhamen; and this is one reason why I was attracted to it, and why the discovery of a new pyramid of this period has drawn so much attention from Egyptologists.

To return to the Step Pyramid of Djoser: the actual burial chamber of the king was not within the pyramid structure itself but cut out of the rock beneath. Imhotep sank a square pit, 21 feet square and 90 feet deep, at the bottom of which was built a burial chamber made of blocks of Assuan granite from Upper Egypt. In the roof of this chamber a hole was made for the introduction of the mummy. Afterward this hole was sealed with a massive granite plug which weighs three and a half tons. The approach to this pit was at a considerable distance to the north, beyond the outer limits of the pyramid itself; it begins in a shallow trench and plunges under the earth to emerge in the pit. Later this was filled up with rubble, as was the pit itself, above the granite roof of the burial chamber.

But the great central pit is only the core of a labyrinth of underground galleries, which branch off from it to east, south and west. The walls of some of these galleries were covered with blue tiles made in imitation of the reed matting which was probably used as partition walls in the king's palace. With their bewildering turns and bifurcations, these galleries riddle the rock like an enormous rabbit warren. They lead to many store chambers in which were found thousands of stone jars and bowls, some of alabaster, many of porphyritic rock, of superb workmanship. Some bore the names of Djoser and others those of his predecessors. In Ancient Egypt wealth was not in cash—currency was unknown—but in grain, oil and other provisions, besides gold and semiprecious stones. The latter have disappeared, plundered by tomb robbers thousands of years ago; but this mighty collection of stone vessels bears eloquent testimony to the power of the king, who commanded the resources of a unified Egypt.

Along the east side of the first mastaba which Imhotep built, he sank a number of shafts, more than 100 feet deep, each ending in a long horizontal gallery running from east to west. These were evidently intended for the tombs and funerary furniture of the queen and other members of the royal family. Within some of them the excavators Firth and Quibell found alabaster sarcophagi and the pedestals on which others had stood. But all these had been robbed.

Soon it was found necessary to incorporate these eastern galleries beneath the main structure of the pyramid, and this seems to have been the reason for the eastward extension of the mastaba. Up to this time the structure, which was comparatively low, was not visible outside the outer enclosing wall, which was 30 feet high. It was then, apparently, that Imhotep's imaginative genius prompted him to raise the building in a series of receding steps or terraces, visible from afar, dominating the landscape as Djoser dominated his kingdom in life.

At this point it is worth considering some of the theories which have been put forward to account for the pyramidal shape of these enormous tombs. Why was such a shape chosen? Did it happen accidentally, in the course of the transformation from a mastaba to a step pyramid? Or was there some religious significance in the pyramid? A number of ingenious suggestions have been advanced. For instance, that great American scholar, Professor J. H. Breasted, has stated:

> The pyramidal form of the king's tomb was of the most sacred significance. The king was buried under the very symbol of the Sun-god, which stood in the holy of holies in the Sun-temple of Heliopolis . . . and when in mountainous proportions the pyramid rose above the king's sepulcher, dominating the royal city below and the valley beyond for many miles, it was the loftiest object which greeted the Sun-god in all the land, and his morning rays glittered on its shining summit long before he scattered the shadows in the dwellings of humbler mortals below.[6]

A lofty and imaginative conception; but is it true? If, as Breasted suggests, the pyramid was a copy of a religious symbol of the Sun-god kept in the temple, it follows that this symbol was also of pyramidal shape. I. E. S. Edwards, in his excellent book, *The Pyramids of Egypt*, adds an interesting reflection.

> A remarkable spectacle may sometimes be seen in the later afternoon of a cloudy winter day at Giza. When standing on the road to Sakkara and gazing westward at the pyramid plateau, it is possible to see the sun's rays

---

[6] J. H. Breasted, *The Development of Religion and Thought in Ancient Egypt*, p. 72.

striking downward through a gap in the clouds at about the same angle as the slope of the Great Pyramid. The impression made on the mind by the scene is that the immaterial prototype and the material replica are here ranged side by side.[7]

Edwards also points out that in the Pyramid Texts, found inscribed on the galleries and chambers of the Fifth and Sixth Dynasty pyramids, passages occur which suggest that the pyramid may have been regarded as a "ladder to the sky." For example Spell 508 of these texts reads:

> *I have trodden those thy rays as a ramp under my feet whereon I mount up to that my mother, the living Uraeus* [8] *on the brow of Re.*

And there is another Spell, No. 523, which reads:

> *Heaven hath strengthened for thee the rays of the sun in order that thou mayest lift thyself to heaven as the eye of Re.*

But do these texts really signify that the pyramid was regarded as a material ladder to the sky? I think not. In my opinion the Pyramid Texts only refer to an immaterial ladder, *e.g.*, the smoke of incense, dust, etc. In constructing his Step Pyramid, Djoser may have intended only setting up a monument which would be higher than those of his predecessors, symbolizing the "Primeval Hill"—a mound emerging above the primordial waters at the start of cre-

---

[7] I. E. S. Edwards, *The Pyramids of Egypt*; London, 1954, p. 234.
[8] The snake symbol signifying dominion over Lower Egypt.

ation. In any case, as we shall see later, the step pyramid
was only a transitory form, and gave place in time to the
true pyramid, which remained the pattern for as long as
buildings of this type were erected in Egypt.

Two thousand years after the first step pyramid was
built, the Pharaohs ruled from Sais in the Delta. There
seems to have been a kind of Renaissance, in which the
monuments of the Old Kingdom, neglected and plundered
for centuries, awakened a new interest. Some were cleared
and repaired, and the ancient art was meticulously copied
and imitated. It was during this period that the Saites
turned their attention to Djoser's pyramid. Unable or un-
willing to penetrate the original entrance to the north,
they drove a new gallery under the structure from the south.
Eventually they found the great pit, and cleared it down
to the level of the roof of the burial chamber. It is through
this comparatively modern gallery—a mere 2,700 years
old—that the present-day visitor enters the pyramid to
view the pit and the roof of the chamber.

You move down this long, sloping, dimly lighted
gallery until suddenly it ends, and there, far below you,
yawns the huge central pit. Above the dark, bat-haunted
roof rests the great bulk of the pyramid. Below you, at the
base of the pit, is the hole in the granite roof of the burial
chamber, lighted from beneath by a concealed lamp. The
granite plug lies beside it. But the chamber is empty.
Almost certainly it had already been robbed when the
Saites found it nearly three thousand years ago. When
Firth entered the chamber he found only one human leg-

bone, perhaps all that remained of the great king. "To be pyramidally extant," wrote Sir Thomas Browne, "is a fallacy in duration."

Outside, on the northern side of the pyramid, is the small walled-in chamber, the serdab, where Firth found the famous seated statue of Djoser which is now in the Cairo Museum. A replica has been put in its place, and the stone eyes still look out through two narrow apertures, as if awaiting the offerings which were brought by the priests nearly five thousand years ago. Also, within the walled-in enclosure are the remains of buildings, some partially reconstructed, which were intended for the use of the king's ka in the life beyond the grave. In the "Sed Festival" ceremony it appears that the king was identified with Osiris, the god of the dead, who was slain and then revivified to live eternally. In the same way the deified king expected that his life would be perpetually renewed. His monument, of shining white limestone, rising above its high enclosing wall, would be a perpetual reminder to his people that their sovereign, now a god, reigned for eternity.

I describe the Step Pyramid of Djoser at some length because, if readers are familiar with its history and construction, they will be in a better position to appreciate the significance of the newly discovered pyramid, which was built by one of the great king's successors. There are certain architectural features which are worth remembering, because they have a direct bearing on the story which follows.

First there is the so-called Southern Tomb of Djoser,

which has puzzled many Egyptologists, and which still remains something of a mystery. Under the southern wall of the enclosure there is a deep shaft, sloping down into the rock and leading to a second tomb, not unlike that beneath the pyramid itself. It consists of a great pit, 21 feet square and 90 feet deep, the same breadth and depth as that under the pyramid itself. Also, like the pyramid tomb, there is a granite chamber at the bottom, but it is smaller than the pyramid chamber, too small to have contained a body. Yet the name of the king appears on the walls of the galleries, together with some fine sculptured reliefs which depict him taking part in the "Sed" ceremonies. In these galleries, as in those beneath the pyramid, parts of the walls are covered with blue glazed tiles in imitation of reed mats.

Why was this second tomb made, if it was indeed a tomb? Some archaeologists have suggested that it may have been intended to accommodate the canopic jars, the four sacred vessels containing the internal organs of the king, removed during the process of embalmment. No such jars have been found, so there is no evidence to prove or disprove this theory. But there is another possibility, which was suggested to me by discoveries made in the new pyramid and which I will discuss in a later chapter.

Then there is the magnificent complex of buildings within the outer enclosure, structures which enable us to see the very beginnings of the art of building in stone. There is the "Sed Festival" court which I have already mentioned, a long rectangular courtyard to the southeast of the pyramid with remains of chapels, each with an open dummy door leading to a small offering-chamber. On the south side of the Sed court two flights of steps lead to a large stone platform, perhaps intended to support a representation of the two thrones of Upper and Lower Egypt.

South of this court is the entrance colonnade, approached by a towered entrance which projects from the outer enclosing wall. This colonnade is long and narrow, bordered with two rows of engaged, fluted columns, the upper parts of which, with the roof, have been restored in recent years. The columns are fasciculated and they seem to have imitated wooden columns which in turn may have been copied from a support made from the stems of reeds bound together. Here again, at each end of the colonnade we find dummy doors of stone made in imitation of wooden doors, even to the ends of the crossbars to which the wooden panels were nailed, all faithfully imitated in stone. Here is proof, if proof were not already available, that this is man's first attempt to build in stone, at a time when the laws of stone construction had not yet imposed themselves, and earlier forms were therefore slavishly copied.

There are within the enclosure, many other buildings which I do not intend to describe here, since readers who are interested can find full details in the works of Firth, Quibell, Lauer, and other authorities.[9] I mention these examples only because they have a direct bearing on the new discoveries. There are, moreover, two additional

---

[9] See C. M. Firth and J. E. Quibell, *The Step Pyramid*; Cairo, 1935.

features of Djoser's monument to which I wish to draw attention.

First, there is the great enclosure wall, which was originally over 30 feet high, and which was decorated with bastions and paneled, in imitation of earlier mud-brick structures. The core was of rubble, encased with small finely massed blocks of smooth white limestone, like the pyramid itself. People often admire the fine jointing of the outer face of these stones, but in fact this occurs only on the surface. Unlike the much larger blocks used in the casing of later pyramids, the joints are not accurately faced throughout their full depth. This great wall, which, when it stood to its full height, must have been a magnificent spectacle, may have imitated the White Walls of Memphis which are mentioned in ancient texts. Scattered irregularly between the bastions are fourteen imitation double gates.

The second architectural peculiarity to be remembered is the inner construction of Djoser's Step Pyramid itself. It is built of independent "skins" of masonry, inclining inward at an angle of 74 degrees and resting on a central core of rubble. This was done to give solidity to the structure. In fact all pyramids, even the true pyramids of Khufu, Khafre and other later kings, were made in this way. There is a difference, however, between the skins or layers of the early step pyramids and those of later times. In a step pyramid the stone courses are laid *at right angles to the facing lines, i.e.,* to the angle of inclination at which the layers leaned on the central core. In later pyramids, which we call "true" pyramids since they were finished with straight sides, the courses were laid *horizontally*.

Step pyramids are characteristic of the Third Dynasty, and similar structures, though in a far more ruined state than that of Djoser, exist at Zawiyet-el-Eryan, between Giza and Sakkara; at Medum, where one of the kings, probably Huni, began building a stepped structure which was afterward completed by Snofru as a true pyramid; at Sila, in the Fayum; at Zawiyet El Mayyitin, in Middle Egypt; at Nubt and at Kula, both in Upper Egypt.

TWO

The Kings of the Third Dynasty

ON MARCH 9, 1951, I WAS TRANSFERRED FROM LUXOR, where I had held the post of Chief Inspector of Antiquities for Upper Egypt and Keeper of the Theban Necropolis, to Sakkara, where I had begun my archaeological career in 1937. At that time I had been Assistant Archaeologist, and had worked for some time on the Causeway of Unis, a Fifth Dynasty king whose pyramid stands not far from that of Djoser. This time I was to be Chief Inspector of Sakkara, responsible for the protection and preservation of all the antiquities in the area. I was glad to have been transferred to Sakkara for a special reason.

For a long period I had been puzzled by the fact that although the Third Dynasty was one of the most important in Egyptian history—the time when Egypt had become a unified kingdom ruled from Memphis—little was known of any of the Third Dynasty kings apart from Djoser. Incidentally this was a later version of his name. It was not used until after his death and is not found before the Twelfth Dynasty (1990–1777 B.C.). On contemporary

27

monuments he is referred to as Horus Nether-er-Khet. He was also called Nether-er-Inhet. He was probably the son and successor of Kha'sekhemui, the last king of the Second Dynasty. Such progress was made in his reign that it can hardly be doubted that his accession marked the beginning of a new era in the history of Egypt, and it was with good reason that he was considered by Manetho as the founder of a new dynasty known as The Third.

He had an earlier tomb, or probably a cenotaph, in the form of a crude brick mastaba, at Bet Khallaf, but it seems certain that he was buried beneath his Step Pyramid at Sakkara. Aided by a number of distinguished men, of whom the most notable was his Chief Architect, Imhotep, he was able not only to consolidate the newly unified kingdom but to imbue it with a new dynamism so that Egyptian civilization flowered afresh. Surviving relics of his reign show radical changes in the arts which could only have been made possible by new and momentous achievements in science. The most notable example, of course, is the monumental complex at Sakkara, which seems to have sprung suddenly into existence with a highly developed architecture for which there is no precedent anywhere in the world. And yet there were other Third Dynasty kings after Djoser. What were their achievements, and where were their monuments?

It was with these thoughts in my mind that one sunny morning in September, 1951, I roved from court to court in Djoser's Step Pyramid enclosure. The pyramid towered above me as I went around to the western side of the structure and sat reflecting in its shade. Could it be, I wondered, that the memory of this great monarch had eclipsed that of his successors in the same way as his pyramid overshadowed the other, lesser monuments in the area? Was it possible that some other kings of that dynasty were also buried here, but that their tombs had long been forgotten?

I ran over in my mind the names of Djoser's successors. Four kings are known to have succeeded him, though Manetho's list is not necessarily complete. These kings, little more than names, are:

(1) Sa-nakht (Neb-ka).
(2) Kha-ba (Teti?).
(3) Nefer-ka (Nebka-re).
(4) Anu (Huni).

Of these known kings, the name of Sa-nakht appears in a crude brick mastaba at Bet Khallaf; Kha-ba may have built the so-called Layer Pyramid at Zawiyet-el-Eryan, between Sakkara and Giza; Nefer-ka probably excavated the unfinished substructure at the same locality; Anu (Huni) began the large pyramid at Medum, which is often ascribed to Snofru who completed it. The presence of "probablys" and "many haves" indicates the vagueness of our knowledge of this period, so different from that of the New Kingdom, in which we can confidently ascribe tombs and monuments to such monarchs as Amenophis III, Rameses II and III, Merneptah, and so on. The reason for this vagueness is partly the fact that, unlike the monuments of later epochs, the very early pyramids were infrequently inscribed with the names of their owners. Where such names occur, they are usually roughly painted on building blocks. Also, these kings were in the habit of building several monuments in different parts of Egypt, and, to complicate matters still further, mastabas containing the names of kings may, in fact, be merely the tombs of high officials who served under those monarchs. For example, some authorities believe that the so-called mastaba of Djoser at Bet Khallaf is actually the tomb of such an official. However, one fact seems certain: pyramids were built for kings and kings alone.

Let us first examine briefly such monuments as can definitely be ascribed to Third Dynasty kings, and which exhibit the same methods of construction as appear in Djoser's pyramid.

At Zawiyet-el-Eryan, a few miles from Sakkara in the Giza direction, are the much-ruined remains of a step pyramid, and, nearby, the approach ramp and deep rock-cut pit seemingly intended for another pyramid which was never built. The first-mentioned monument, ascribed to Kha-ba, has a core of limestone against which lean fourteen layers or skins of masonry of the same material. It is about 300 feet square and at present about 60 feet high. The sarcophagus chamber is cut out of the rock beneath the structure and approached by a stairway and passage from an entrance on the northeast side. Outside the pyramid, on its north-northeast and northwest sides, was a long rock-cut corridor with thirty-two recesses or storage chambers.

The unfinished example on the north consists merely of a long descending passage, over 300 feet in length, with a double stairway cut out of the rock. This begins with a slight slope, then becomes level, and finally plunges down at a steep angle until it opens into an enormous square pit not unlike that beneath Djoser's pyramid. At the bottom, no doubt, the intention was to build a granite burial chamber, and the blocks still lie there, some of them roughly painted with the name Nebka-re or Nefer-ka. There is also a magnificent sarcophagus of red granite, lying where it was left nearly five thousand years ago. But the great shaft and its approach ramp lie open to the sky, and the pyramid which was to have covered them was never finished.[1]

There remains the south pyramid at Medum, begun by Huni (Anu), the last king of the Third Dynasty.[2] The Medium pyramid dominates the landscape for miles around; in fact, there are few monuments in the whole of Egypt more impressive than this steep-sided, towerlike structure, with sides only a few degrees off the vertical, rising out of a high mound of sand like a mediaeval keep on a hilltop. But what we see is only the mere core of the building, which, when completed, was a *true* pyramid, about 300 feet high and 450 feet square, with a slope-angle of 51 degrees 52 minutes. All the outer casing was

---

[1] Recently (1954) an American film company cleared the thousands of tons of sand which filled the pit in order to "shoot" scenes of pyramid building, so that the granite blocks and the sarcophagus are temporarily visible for the first time in many years.

[2] Previously believed to have been built by Snofru. Now, however, attributed to Huni and probably finished by Snofru. See Hayes, *The Sceptre of Egypt*; New York, 1954.

removed centuries ago, together with most of the upper part of the outer accretion-layers, leaving only the innermost layers visible. The rest is covered with sand and rubble. But this spoliation has had one advantage—the building shows more clearly than any other the *inner construction* of a pyramid.

Against a central core of rubble the architect laid the layers of masonry, each leaning inward at an angle of 73–75 degrees, the innermost layer being the highest, the next one lower, the next one lower still, and so on, so that the building presented the appearance of a flight of seven or eight mighty steps. But afterward the king or his architect appears to have been dissatisfied, so the spaces between the steps were filled in and cased with fine limestone. Thus we can see in the pyramid at Medum, monument to the last king of the Third Dynasty, two stages in the development of the pyramid, first, the step pyramid, and second, the true pyramid.

To return now to Sakkara: it seemed strange to me that in this, the most important necropolis of Memphis, there is only one monument which can definitely be ascribed to a Third Dynasty king. Where, for example, was the pyramid of Sa-nakht? And for all we know there may have been other kings of the Third Dynasty not mentioned in the lists. I resolved to make a minute examination of the necropolis, from north to south and from east to west.

If readers will try to fix in their minds the principal features of the area, it will help them to understand the thought processes which led me to dig at a certain spot. The necropolis extends around the desert to the west of Memphis for about four and a half miles from north to south, the maximum width from east to west being about one mile. It is a rocky plateau about 120 feet high, covered with sand, and was used for burial from the early dynastic period right down to the period of the Arab Conquest in the seventh century A.D.—that is, for more than four thousand years. After the Conquest, Memphis was gradually deserted, as the new city of Al-Fustat was founded on the other side of the river near the modern site of Cairo. The stones of the old capital were transported across the river and re-used for building the new city.

Starting our exploration in the extreme north, we find first the great tombs of the First and Second Dynasties and brick mastaba of the Third Dynasty. Also there are brick and stone mastaba of the Fourth and Fifth Dynasties, stretching from east to west in the northern part of the necropolis.

Moving southward we come to the Avenue of Sphinxes, built by King Nectanebo of the Thirtieth Dynasty (378–332 B.C.), leading from the edge of the cultivation to the Serapeum, where the sacred Apis Bulls were buried throughout the period extending from the Eighteenth Dynasty (1555–1350 B.C.) to the end of the Ptolemaic period. Outside the Serapeum there was a semicircle of statues of Greek poets and philosophers, discovered by the French archaeologist Mariette in the last century. Near this place stands the huge mastaba of

Thy, and other large and impressive tombs of nobles, priests, and officials of the Old Kingdom.

Still moving southward we come to the Pyramids of Teti (Dyn. VI) and Userkhaf (Dyn. V), both in a sadly ruined condition. Then Djoser's Step Pyramid, with its accompanying complex of buildings surrounded by its wall, and a little farther to the south the pyramid complex of Unis, a Fifth Dynasty king. South of this, at some distance, is the ruined Pyramid of Pepy I (Dyn. VI); then, after another expanse of desert, the Pyramids of Merenré (Dyn. VI) and Djedkare (Dyn. V), from which point you can see, some miles farther south, a cluster of pyramids which mark the southern limits of the Sakkara Necropolis. These are the monuments of Pepy II (Dyn. VI), his queens, Neit and Iput, and other small subsidiary pyramids. Near the Pyramid of Pepy II is an extraordinary monument which goes by the name of Mastabat Faraûn. This, although it is rectangular, has in its substructure many of the characteristics of a pyramid. Some scholars believe that its shape reproduces that of an enormous sarcophagus. It was the tomb of King Shepsekaf, the last king of the Fourth Dynasty.

These great and enduring monuments, seen far off across the desert at glaring noonday, or from the roof of my house at midnight, mysterious in the moonlight, are the daily companions of my work. I know them all, and they are like old friends to me. Even their names are beautiful: "Pure is Shepsekaf"; "Enduring are the Places of Teti"; "Beautiful are the Places of Unis"; "Snofru Appears"; and I hope I will not be accused of romanticism when I say that they have been an inspiration to me in my work. All of them have been excavated, at some time or other, by great archaeologists of the past, such as Maspero, Firth and Jequier; and all were found to have been robbed, or partially robbed, in remote antiquity. The Ancient Egyptian tomb robber was a zealous and cunning worker, and few are the tombs that have escaped him! And yet one could not be an archaeologist without faith and hope, and as I wandered around my domain during those first few months after my appointment, I kept returning to the problem of the unknown monuments of the Third Dynasty kings.

It was true that Sakkara had been dug many, many times; excavations were begun more than a century ago by Mariette, and afterward Jacques de Morgan, another French archaeologist, took up Mariette's work in a more scientific manner. But no really systematic work was started until the present century, when the Egyptian Antiquities Department began a careful scientific exploration of the whole area.

I was the latest of a long line of archaeologists who had worked at Sakkara, and I would not have been human if I had not hoped that to me would be granted the opportunity of making further discoveries. After a careful examination of the whole necropolis, I was finally drawn to a section which lies behind Djoser's enclosure. This is a vast area, bounded on the east by Djoser's western wall and the Pyramid of Unis, and on the west by the great enclosure found by Jacques de Morgan half a century ago, and subsequently worked on for one season by the late Abdessalam Hussein. The most conspicuous feature of this area is the presence in its southeast corner of a vast oblong terrace lying at a distance of about 450 feet to the southwest of Djoser's enclosure and extending from north to south.

This terrace was marked on the maps as a natural plateau, but its peculiar character, covered as it was with fragments of worked limestone, granite and alabaster, and with occasional outcroppings of rubble masonry, puzzled and intrigued me. I approached my Department with a request to make trial excavations there. To my delight I was given a preliminary grant of £600, and on September 27th, 1951, I began my excavations.

THREE

I Begin My Search

READERS WHO ARE UNFAMILIAR WITH ARCHAEOLOGICAL work may like to know how an operation such as this is organized. The site having been chosen, the next step is to recruit suitable workmen. Controlled, careful digging calls for considerable skill; the men must know what they are looking for, be experienced in identifying various types of walls, embankments, and minute evidences of the presence of former buildings, and be expert in observing archaeological evidence which would pass unnoticed by the untrained eye. Equally important, they must know how to handle with the utmost care the delicate and fragile objects of antiquity which may come to light in the course of the excavations and how to apply the necessary preservative treatment. Also, of course, they must be scrupulously honest, for the temptation to pocket small objects is strong.

Fortunately for the Egyptian archaeologist, in a village in Upper Egypt named Koptos there are men who specialize in this kind of work. They are drawn from the peasant class, but they have been trained in scientific digging by archaeologists, and have made this their principal occupation. Some of the older ones received their training fifty years ago from such men as Sir William Flinders Petrie, and they in turn have trained others. For instance, my *reis*, or chief workman, Hofni Ibrahim, has worked for the archaeologists Petrie, Brunton, Myers, Baily, Starkie, Miss Caton-Thompson, and more recently Professor Fairman. The experience of such men is invaluable to any excavator tackling a new site, and I was fortunate enough to be able to recruit several to assist me in my task.

It is interesting that this work runs in whole families —fathers, sons, uncles, nephews, cousins, all expert diggers. And it is a point of honor among them always to be loyal and honest, since if one member is guilty of carelessness or dishonesty, the whole family is disgraced.

Although they work for wages, these men are much more than mere hired laborers. They take a genuine interest in their work, and will talk proudly of the discoveries they have made under the leadership of famous archaeologists who have employed them. These people, after all, are the lineal descendants of the Ancient Egyptians, and have inherited many of their beliefs and customs. They work among the monuments which their ancestors built, and it would seem that some of the ancient skills have descended to them—for instance, an extraordinary facility in moving heavy objects with little mechanical assistance. An English friend told me how he watched with amazement and trepidation the moving of a granite colossus in the Cairo Museum, a statue weighing perhaps a hundred tons. "A few wiry little chaps in *gallabliyehs*," he said, "gathered around the statue with iron levers and a few balks of timber. There was an awful lot of shouting and heaving, the thing began to rock and catastrophe seemed imminent. I felt like shutting my eyes and stuffing my fingers in my ears, but in a short time the colossus was shifted several yards and ended up in its new position quite unharmed." This was an ancient art which had been handed down.

When I was at Luxor as Chief Inspector for Upper Egypt, I employed several of these men. Two in particular were extremely skillful and responsible—the brothers Hofni Ibrahim and Hussein Ibrahim. I wrote to Hofni, who was at Koptos, in Upper Egypt, and discovered that he was on the point of going to work in the Sudan. However, both he and his brother preferred to work in Egypt, even in Lower Egypt far from their homes; so I was delighted when they agreed to join me at Sakkara, bringing with them ten other hand-picked men. I appointed Hofni Ibrahim my *reis* and supplemented the skilled labor force with twenty local workmen for the rougher work, though I knew that later I should have to recruit more men.

During the last few days of September, 1951, Hofni and I went around the vast site looking for a suitable place to begin work. Our attention was drawn to an outcropping of rubble masonry just appearing above the surface on the western border of the terrace. So we began to dig at this point. To our delight, on the first day a massive wall of rubble-coursed masonry appeared. We dug down to the bottom of the wall, which was about 17 feet deep, and found that it was built on the rock and had a thickness of over 60 feet. It was built in three parts, like a sandwich. The middle of the sandwich was an upright course about 11 feet thick, faced on each side with another course; the outer sides of which sloped inward at an angle of 72 degrees. Architects call this type of construction a "battered" wall.

This discovery reassured me that my original conception was correct, and during the following two months we continued to make further excavations at points along the length of this massive wall. I increased my gang of workmen to fifty. Under Hofni Ibrahim's direction, the "Decauville" railway was laid down to carry the excavated sand and rock from the site to a suitable dumping place. The terrace lies in the southeast corner of the great depression, which is situated to the southwest of Djoser's enclosure. I chose as my dumping ground an area to the west of the west border of the terrace, having first examined the place by digging other trial pits to make sure that it was only rock strata and did not conceal tombs or monuments. The "Decauville" is a light, narrow-gauge railway which can be rapidly laid down and equally rapidly removed to a new site when required. Steel tip-trucks run along it, and the rumble of these, mingled with the songs and rhythmic chanting of the workmen, is a sound with which all Egyptian archaeologists are familiar. It is music to the excavator's heart!

The wall was built of large uniform blocks of local

gray limestone, and the upper part appeared to have been quarried in antiquity. When I had defined this wall, I searched for the corners, and eventually established the limits. I found that it was built around a rectangular enclosure, which had a north-south axis of about 1,700 feet and an east-west axis of about 600 feet.

The enormous thickness of this wall and the fact that it was not faced with fine limestone, as was Djoser's circuit wall, puzzled me at first. Then I realized that it was really a foundation platform on which the upper wall had originally been built. The lay of the land showed why this was. Djoser's pyramid complex stands on a commanding site on the very edge of the plateau, overlooking the valley; but the king for whom the newly discovered enclosure was built did not have this advantage. His monument had to be built in a depression, and in order to overcome this his architect had first built this massive stone platform of local limestone, which would not perhaps be visible to the eye, and on top of it he had built the *real* enclosure wall, of similar type to that of Djoser, with projecting bastions and probably dummy gates, all of which would be visible from afar. Most of this curtain wall had disappeared; the fine limestone of which it was built had been too great a temptation to subsequent builders. The kings of Ancient Egypt frequently plundered their ancestors' monuments, and this wall had fallen a victim like the rest. Nevertheless, I had no doubt that the uppermost wall had been completed, because we came across several fragments of it in the extreme northern limit of the enclosure, with paneled bastions and "curtains," [1] having the same measurements as those of Djoser's wall. This, incidentally, is one of the reasons why I believe that the king who built this enclosure was later than Djoser, since, if that king's monument had not already existed, the builders of this other structure would have raised it nearer to the edge of the plateau, not only because of the more advantageous position, but because they would have been nearer the western bank of the Nile, at which the facing stones would have to be unloaded. For although the cores of the pyramids were built of local limestone, the fine-grained stone needed for the facing blocks was quarried from the hills on the eastern bank of the Nile.

Further excavations in the northern area of the rectangular terrace revealed several rubble walls, running parallel with one another in an east-west direction, and joined together with small cross-walls, also of rubble, the whole strikingly resembling some of the embankments and fillings in Djoser's enclosure. It took us about two months to excavate and examine this bewildering complex of cross-walls, for it was difficult to know where to begin digging in this vast enclosure. I must emphasize at this point the immensity of the place. It was not like excavating a simple tomb in a small circumscribed spot, but comparable to digging throughout an area several times the size of Trafalgar Square in London. Dozens of times I went with Hofni Ibrahim to re-examine Djoser's enclosure,

---

[1] "Curtains": wall-faces between the bastions.

particularly at its northern end, in the hope of finding clues to the layout of the newly discovered enclosure. We found the same complex of walls in several places, but chiefly in the northern end.

The reason for the existence of these cross-walls was as follows: when the builders of that remote period wished to raise the level of an area, they first built cross-walls, dividing the area into compartments which they afterward filled in with stone. Also, it is very important to remember that the buildings in Djoser's enclosure were not real buildings intended for human habitation, but dummies. They were practically solid, and these walls were used in the construction of such dummy structures.

Let me put it this way. If one is excavating, say, a house or a temple, one can tell which were walls and which were spaces between the walls for chambers. But in this case the spaces left within the structures were so small that the whole construction looked as if it was one solid mass. Most of these buildings were, in fact, symbolic, designed to represent certain elements in the king's palace at Memphis which were deemed necessary for his habitation in the after-life and for him to assert his rights of sovereignty.

The difficulty of establishing the layout of such buildings when they have been reduced to foundation level can be imagined, and this was why I returned frequently to the enclosure of Djoser, which had been systematically excavated, to see if I could gain information which would enable me to interpret the layout of the new structure.

The resemblances were striking, and I became increasingly convinced that this was indeed the enclosure of a step pyramid, though at the time few others believed me.

In work of this kind the archaeologist sometimes runs into blind alleys—both literally and figuratively—and one such distraction occurred while we were digging in this area. We noticed that most of the fragments used in the fillings were chips of soft clay, called in Arabic *tafl*, which are usually found in the debris from subterranean galleries. This led us to suspect that there might be subterranean galleries underneath, perhaps leading to tombs, the more so since similar complexes of walls are found over such galleries in the northern part of Djoser's enclosure. So we searched for the entrance, and I remembered my two chief workmen and I spent a long time conjecturing where it might be. The other workmen joined enthusiastically in the search, and, as usually happens on such occasions, each had his own special theory. Cries would go up "The entrance is here!" . . . "No, it is here!" and so on, and every day brought new conjectures. It was very difficult to see one's way out of this maze, particularly as visitors and other archaeologists came to see us, and, after viewing the site, expressed the opinion that the enclosure had never been completed and that we would find nothing.

The search for a tomb having proved vain, I decided at last to shift the whole work a few yards farther north. It was at Christmas, 1951, that I told *Reis* Hofni to move the Decauville railway to the north of this complex and attack the high terrace immediately to the north. Imagine our joy when, on New Year's Day, 1952, we suddenly found a flight of steps leading to an enormous cross-wall, which ran from east to west across the enclosure. This wall was quite different from those I had discovered earlier. It was faced with fine white limestone and built with bastions and curtains just like those of Djoser's enclosure wall. Also it was similarly paneled. For some reason it had never been completed and had been embedded in a mass of dry masonry composed of rubble cross-walls built at intervals over and against its bastions and curtains, the gaps being filled up with debris. The wall was found intact to the length of 138 feet at the very stage when its construction was broken off, probably because of an alteration in the architect's design. As it gradually revealed itself in all its beauty, exactly as the workmen had left it nearly five thousand years ago, I realized that here was a find of major importance.

FOUR

The White Wall

THE NEW YEAR SEEMED FULL OF HOPE FOR US ALL.
Hofni, his brother, and the rest of the workmen were as
delighted as I was. In the past they had worked on some
great excavations, and it was a point of honor for them
that at every site on which they worked something important should be found. Naturally such expectations are
not always realized, and when they are there is great re-
joicing. Such experiences then became part of their life
history, which they tell to their children.

Perhaps some readers will wonder why such a fuss
should be made over a mere stone wall. But this was no
ordinary wall. It is very rare in Egypt to find such a structure untouched by time, and as we cleared more and more
of its length we found incontestable evidence that the
White Wall, as we named it, must have been buried very
shortly after its construction. We were looking at something which no human eye had seen for nearly fifty
centuries.

This evidence consisted of marks and drawings in red
paint left on the white limestone surface by the ancient
builders. For instance, on some of the stone blocks were

quarry marks, painted on the stones before they left the quarries on the opposite side of the Nile. Those on the White Wall were mere symbols of which the meaning is lost, but we know from other examples found in the later pyramids that some of these marks indicated the names of the gangs or crews who cut the stone. These crews are believed to have consisted of some eight hundred to a thousand men. For instance, here are the names of some of the crews who quarried stone for the pyramids of Cheops and Mycerinus:

The crew, Cheops excites love.
The crew, the White Crown of Khnmw-Khufu
    (Cheops) is powerful.
The crew, Sahure is beloved.

Other marks have been translated as follows:

This side up.
To be taken away.
For the royal tomb.

These roughly drawn signs and inscriptions bring one very close to the ancient builders. On the White Wall, for example, we found the actual leveling-lines, made by stretching a cord dipped in red paint across the surface and "flipping" it, just as a modern mason does to this day. These were evidently made to ensure that workmen should lay the stones at the same level along the entire length of the wall. Even though this was perhaps only the second or third attempt at building monumental walls in stone masonry, the builders had evidently acquired great skill.

Then we found something which brought the remote past very near to us: human touches on a royal Egyptian monument. Here and there the ancient workmen had beguiled a leisure moment by drawing on the wall, in red ocher or lampblack, pictures of men, animals and boats. There was a figure of a Libyan man in a long robe and tall headdress, carrying a bow. The Libyans, nomads living in the West Desert, were, of course, foreigners to the Egyptians whose dress was quite dissimilar. Then there were unmistakable drawings of lions. At that time lions and other beasts of prey were still found in the deserts of Egypt, and the men must have seen them many times roaming the desert fringes. Other drawings showed boats, some with sails and some without, and barges similar to those which were used by the Ancient Egyptians to bring blocks of limestone from the eastern bank of the Nile.

With these memorials of the ancient workmen before us, let us consider for a moment some of the methods used by the Ancient Egyptians in the quarrying and use of stone. This is a vast subject, about which many volumes have been written. I shall return to it in a later chapter when I come to discuss the building of pyramids; meanwhile here are a few facts concerning Egyptian masonry at this very early period, when man first learned to build monumentally in stone.

From the Third Dynasty onward the Egyptians obtained much of their fine-grained limestone from quarries in the eastern cliffs of the Nile opposite Memphis. Two quarries in particular were famous: Tura and Masura. These supplied the fine limestone used for casing the monuments. Usually the inner core of masonry, where extreme hardness was not necessary, came from quarries as near as possible to the building under construction. There are such quarries adjacent to Sakkara and near the pyramids of Giza.

Nowadays, of course, stone is first blasted from the solid rock by explosives, and afterward cut and shaped in the mason's yard. The Ancient Egyptians, having no such facilities, had to rely on muscle power and simple tools. In the actual quarries at Tura and elsewhere you may see to this day how they quarried the stone and shaped it on the spot. The quarries are wide horizontal galleries cut out of the rock. Some of them are hundreds of feet deep, with massive columns of natural rock purposely left by the quarrymen to support the roof. The workmen started at the top of the rock wall and worked downward. First they hollowed out a ledge along which a man might crawl. Then, with a mason's pick or perhaps a copper chisel, he would cut out grooves at the back and sides, leaving a rough block of stone still attached at its base to the parent rock. Finally, a few sharp blows at the base with a hammer and chisel would release the block. This process would be continued along the length of the ledge, and then the men would commence chiseling downward to remove the next course.

Even hard stones like granite were quarried in this manner, though in such quarries, instead of splitting the rock from its base with a hammer and chisel, which would have been impossible, the workmen drove slots into the rock, into which they inserted metal wedges to which powerful hammer blows were applied. Another method was to pack these slots with wooden wedges which were soaked in water. The wood then expanded and split the rock.[1]

Thus the stone blocks came from the quarry already roughly shaped, and needed only final squaring to make them ready for use in the wall or monument. However, the final dressing was usually done near the building itself, and the facing not until after the blocks had been laid. To test their smoothness, the masons used a facing-plate dipped in red paint which left a mark on the "high spots." For shaping the blocks the workmen used copper chisels. Incidentally the oft-quoted statement that the Ancient Egyptians knew the secret of hardening copper is a fallacy. Such chisels as have been found had been annealed but not to any extraordinary hardness, and the waste of metal must have been enormous.

For establishing a level base-line at the foundation, they ran a watercourse along and around the surface to be leveled, "then measured down from the surface at many points simultaneously, thus establishing datum points to which the complete surface would eventually be reduced"

---

[1] For a full account of this fascinating and little-known subject, see S. Clarke and R. Engelbach, *Ancient Egyptian Masonry*; Oxford University Press, 1930, pp. 12–33.

(Engelbach). This, by the way, would explain the slight error which exists in the level of the platform which runs partly under the Great Pyramid at Giza. It is on a perfect plane, but slopes up about 6 inches from the northeast to the southwest corner. If, when the points were being checked, a northeast wind had been blowing, this would have produced the error.

Other instruments which were used at this period were the plumb line, examples of which have been found, and the set-square.

The unit of measurement used during the Old and Middle Kingdoms was the royal cubit; the hieroglyphic sign for this is an outstretched arm, which is the approximate length of 1 cubit (20.612 inches). This in turn was divided into seven palms, each of which had four fingers. Sometimes we find markings in cubits behind the casing stones of pyramids and on unfinished walls of temples and tombs. There must also, of course, have been architect's drawings, and though none have been found dating from the Third Dynasty,[2] later examples exist: for example, a plan on limestone of the tomb of Rameses IX, from the Valley of Kings at Thebes, which can be seen in the Cairo Museum.

It would seem that the work of quarrying, transporting the stones, and building the monuments took place at certain specific periods of the year. Quarrying of fine white

---

[2] However, a diagram of the Third Dynasty with lineal measures drawn in red ink on a limestone flake was found in Djoser's enclosure. This is probably a working diagram supplying data for building a curved wall as it defines a curve with co-ordinates. It is now in the Cairo Museum.

limestone took place usually in winter and spring (November to March). The stones would be transported across the river during the season of the inundation, the annual flooding of the Nile (July-November), when the river was at its widest. This was done in order to reduce surface haulage to a minimum. Therefore building is likely to have been most active during the months following the inundation, when the work of transportation was over and the summer heat had abated.

I must repeat at this point that no evidence had so far been uncovered to indicate that I had found a pyramid. I had found an enclosure which bore certain resemblances to that of King Djoser, and a magnificent cross-wall which was so like that king's enclosure wall as to leave no doubt that it must have been built at a period very close to Djoser. But that was all. Apart from the White Wall, visitors to the site in those early months of 1952 found little to impress them, only the bare plateau, of sand and rock, pitted with a few holes, from one of which the Decauville ran to the rubbish dump. "Where's the pyramid?" my professional colleagues would ask jocularly, and I had no answer—only an inner faith that somewhere beneath that vast expanse of sand I would eventually find what I was looking for. But when I thought of my modest and rapidly dwindling allowance I became anxious, for if the money was spent on fruitless digging it might be difficult to obtain more. The site of each trial pit would have to be chosen with great care, and night after night, when

The White Wall

I returned to my house after the day's work, I would study the plan of the area, consult the works of other archaeologists who had worked on pyramids, form and reject theories, and talk far into the night with my chief workmen, Hofni and Hussein.

At this stage I would like to refer my readers again to the plan of the pyramid enclosure. They will notice that north of the point where the White Wall joins the north-south walls of the enclosure there is a curious change of alignment. We discovered this shortly after the wall was revealed, and it puzzled me for some time. In fact, there were two features which gave me cause for thought. First there was the fact that, from the White Wall onward, in a northerly direction, the east-west walls of the enclosure did not follow the same line as before, but were inset to a depth of about 6 feet, forming an angle. This indicated either another monument attached to the first, on the northern side, or else *an extension of the original monument*. Later I found that this latter supposition was correct.

The second strange feature was that this northern extension, beyond the White Wall, was raised above the level of the southern part of the enclosure, forming a kind of raised platform. Why was this done? Only further excavation will provide a final answer.

In the meantime, in an endeavor to find an answer to the puzzle, I began to excavate the whole breadth of the enclosure from west to east, following the line of the White Wall. We first encountered large blocks of fine limestone so arranged as to form a flight of steps built at the western end of the massive wall, and designed to facilitate its exploitation as a quarry.

The wall itself proved to be comprised of a thick, regularly built inner core of local limestone, faced outside with dressed white limestone. The whole outer face of the wall was paneled and constructed with bastions and curtains. The whole magnificent structure presented exactly the same design as Djoser's enclosure wall. The panels had the same breadth and depth. The bastions and curtains had the same measurements, with equal spaces in the larger bastions for carving imitation closed double gates, as in Djoser's wall. I was delighted, because it was now clear that I had found an enclosure built on similar lines to that of Djoser.

Throughout the rest of the 1952 working season, from January to March, we continued to excavate this wall, stopping only when we found that at its eastern end, nearest to the necropolis, it had been damaged by quarrying.

However, we noticed two essential differences in the structural disposition of the stones. The dimensions of the stones here were much larger than those of Djoser's enclosure; in the new wall, the height of the course is about 20 inches, while in the lower parts of Djoser's wall it is 11 to 12 inches. On the other hand, the fine limestone was employed much more thriftily in the casing.

These two factors are extremely important in the dating of the monument. It is certain that already in Djoser's reign there had been a tendency to increase the

size of the stone blocks,[3] as the builders ultimately came
to learn that an increase in size meant an economy in the
work of cutting out the stones, and lent more strength and
a greater degree of cohesion to walls. Therefore the size
of the stones and the way in which they were used in this
new wall suggest a date *later* than Djoser, although still
Third Dynasty. The economy of the casing also suggests
a more rational, hence more developed, method of construction. But the wall had been abandoned during construction, and the northern limit of the enclosure had been
moved 600 feet farther north. That it was abandoned
during construction is proved by the fact that the sixth
and uppermost course had not been faced but had been
left rough. In addition, several partition walls of coarse
limestone leaned directly against the paneled façade, and
the surface of the wall had not been smoothed, but bore
the numerous quarry marks and mason's lines which I have
already described.

Throughout this time my workmen and I still kept a
lookout for signs of subterranean galleries such as exist
beneath the northern part of Djoser's enclosure, and one
day we found something which raised our hopes. It was
a hole made by one of the ancient tomb robbers. To the
archaeologist such holes can be a cause of both hope and
despair. Hope, because they indicate that, thousands of

---

[3] J. P. Lauer, *Les Problèmes des Pyramides d'Egypte*, Paris, 1952, p.
163; Clarke and Engelbach, *Ancient Egyptian Masonry*, Oxford University
Press, 1930, p. 8.

years ago, some enterprising rascal had known or suspected that there was a tomb nearby; despair, lest he should have found and plundered it!

In this case hope triumphed. We went down the hole and followed the robber's tunnel for a distance of 62 feet. It plunged down into the rock and described a wide semicircle. We had to proceed carefully for fear of falling rock or a total collapse of the tunnel, but when Hofni and I reached the end and found only the rock we were delighted and relieved. On this occasion the robber had drawn a blank and given up in disgust. But had he perhaps succeeded elsewhere? The answer to that question still lay in the future.

FIVE

We Find the Pyramid

THE PERIOD FROM JANUARY TO THE BEGINNING OF APRIL,
1952, was spent in clearing the White Wall down to its
base, and along its length to the point where quarrying
had damaged much of the structure. During this time
the layout of the enclosure had become somewhat clearer
to me. When I am excavating a site I always try to identify
myself with the ancient builders, to get inside their minds
in order to understand *why* their monument assumed its
present shape. They often changed their plans during
construction, and by observation and reflection, and by
drawing on one's knowledge of other monuments, it is
sometimes possible to estimate where and why such
changes have occurred, and to make an intelligent guess at
what may lie under the sand at a particular point.

For instance, I became fairly certain that the White
Wall had originally formed the northern limit of the enclosure, but that for some reason not yet explained the
builders decided to extend it to the north at a higher level.
Also, that since this was clearly an enclosure, it must have
had a central edifice, which should be near the geometrical
center of the *original* enclosure. It could be objected that

the builders might have abandoned the enclosure before beginning the central edifice, whatever it was—pyramid or mastaba; but this was unlikely, since we know from other structures that the building of the various component parts went on at one and the same time. But there was no sign of any such central edifice, not even an outcropping of masonry such as had guided me to the enclosure wall.

Early in April, I surveyed the original enclosure with a theodolite in order to determine its exact geometrical center. I explained to Hofni my idea, and he showed an enthusiastic interest. He had not worked before on pyramids of this very early date, though he had played an important part in the excavation of the famous Pyramid of King Senusret II (Dyn. XII) at el-Lahun. In fact, it was Hofni Ibrahim who found one of the most beautiful objects ever discovered in an Egyptian pyramid. In 1914 he was working for Sir Flinders Petrie in the tomb of Princess Sit-Hathor-Junet, daughter of Senusret II, when, during the clearing of a recess in the corner of the tomb he found a rare specimen of the royal Uraeus or sacred snake, in gold, with a head of lapis lazuli, eyes of garnet, and hood ornamented with carnelian, turquoise, and lazuli. This royal symbol, signifying dominion over Lower Egypt, was worn by the Pharaohs in their crowns. Embedded in mud, it had been overlooked by the tomb robbers when they rifled the tomb, and had remained untouched for four thousand years until Hofni found it. He once told me that he often visits the Cairo Museum just to admire the Uraeus in its glass case, and to recall that day, so many years ago, when he first held it in his hands. It is memories such as this which lend glory to the lives of these men, and inspire them with hope whenever they tackle a new site. So it was with considerable excitement that my workmen began the next phase of the excavation, which was to try to locate the central edifice, if it existed.

In all work of this kind luck and judgment both play their part, and on this occasion we were lucky. I had established the spot where the central building should lie, but when I gave instructions for the sinking of the first trial pit I had no idea whether we should strike the edge of the structure or some point within it. Judge of my satisfaction when on January 29, 1952, Hofni came to me excitedly and said that they had found masonry. By good fortune we had located the actual southern edge of the hidden structure, from which point it would not be difficult to follow it along to its corners, and define the limits of the whole edifice.

It proved to be composed of a series of independent walls leaning one on the other and inclining inward at an angle of about 75 degrees, and *the stone courses were at right angles to the slope of the walls.* Readers who have carefully followed Chapter One, in which I described the construction of step pyramids, will realize that this was a valuable clue to the age of the structure. For in the few surviving examples of step pyramids which we know, the accretion walls are built in this manner, whereas in later pyramids built subsequent to the time of Snofru the courses were laid horizontally. I immediately went to Monsieur

Lauer, the architect of the Antiquities Department who has worked for many years on Djoser's Step Pyramid. (He is responsible for restoration and consolidation of monuments.) I found him as usual at work near this pyramid, and together we made our way to the terrace where Hofni, Hussein, and the other workmen were clearing the newly discovered walls. When he had seen and examined them he said to me, "I have no doubt whatsoever that this forms part of a step pyramid."

Even so there were still many who doubted, and unfortunately we had now come to the end of the 1952 season. I knew it would be some time before these doubts could be finally resolved, as I was sure they would be. Excavations closed down in May, 1952, and were not resumed until November, 1953. Work had reached a critical point, and I felt I needed time to study the finds and decide carefully on my next course of action. It was also necessary to obtain an additional grant in order that the work could continue.

In November, 1953, I reassembled my workmen, and once again the loaded trucks began to rumble along the Decauville as we labored to uncover more of this mysterious building. I first concentrated my attention on finding its limits. We extended the pit and assured ourselves that the structure continued on both the east and west sides. Then I gave orders to shift the work some distance to the west on the same line, at a point where I judged the corner of the building might be. We found that the southern side was covered up with soft clay resulting from the cutting of subterranean galleries, so this almost imperceptible evidence showed where the artificial fillings ended and the debris resulting from later quarrying of the pyramid began. When we dug below the desert surface, it was clear where this intentional covering material ended. Not long after this work was begun, I was engaged at another point in the enclosure when Hussein Ibrahim, the brother of Hofni, came running toward me with outstretched arms and crying: "*Mabruk elnasia!*" which means: "Congratulations! We have found the corner!"

I went back with him and found to my joy that they had struck the corner of a pyramid, for this I was now convinced it was. It could hardly have been a mastaba, partly because of its size but chiefly because no mastabas are known to exist with "accretion walls" and inclined courses. These are typical of pyramid construction.

Every archaeological site has its own characteristics, and one has to work for a very long time to identify them and to recognize what happened in ancient times. Because of the immense surface covered by the enclosure, I adopted the method of finding first the main points; otherwise I would have had to expend much time and money on fruitless labor before being able to understand the layout.

For example, after uncovering this first corner it was easy for us to find the other three. From illustration 11 it will be seen that this was a stepped structure, but that only one step remains. The masonry is of good quality, but the limestone blocks are relatively small, as in Djoser's pyramid. The builders had not yet reached the stage when they built with huge megalithic blocks. The whole structure is 400 feet square; the base thus presented is larger than that of Djoser's pyramid. In its unfinished state it has a maximum height of about 23 feet, but I believe that it might have been completed to double this height and that it has been reduced by quarrying in later times. No traces of an outer casing were found, and it may be assumed that only the core of the pyramid was begun and that it was never finished.

This is a square layer-structure consisting of probably fourteen skins of masonry which diminished in height from the center outward and leaned on a central nucleus at an angle varying between 71 and 75 degrees, with the beds of the courses at right angles to the facing lines. The "accretion faces" were left in the rough. Assuming that each pair of these skins of masonry was designed to form one step, as is the case in Djoser's pyramid, we may infer that the new pyramid was intended to have seven steps in place of Djoser's six.

Had this pyramid been finished, it would probably have stood to a height of about 230 feet, i.e., 30 feet higher than Djoser's. It stands directly on the rock, and was built of local, coarse gray limestone. The blocks are roughly squared and are set in a mortar composed of soft clay (tafl) obtained from the tunneling of underground passages, mixed with limestone chips. The stones were generally laid in alternate courses of "headers and stretchers" in imitation of mud-bricks. The courses are level and parallel, and the bedding joints are much wider than the rising joints. A fragment of a boundary stele bearing the name of Djoser was found re-used in the masonry, a further indication that the new pyramid must have been built at a later date than Djoser's.

This kind of structure is characteristic of the so-called step pyramids. Both the Step Pyramid of Djoser and the Layer Pyramid of Zawiyet-el-Eryan are of the same formation (12 layers, inclining at an angle of 74 degrees, in the first,[1] and 14 layers, inclining at an angle of 68 degrees, in the second).[2] The Medum Pyramid has also the same formation in the first and second stages of the superstructure (7 and 8 layers, respectively, and an incline of about 74 degrees).[3] Djoser's original mastaba at Sakkara, which formed the initial core of the superstructure, was built in independent layers of horizontal courses.[4] But when the design of a "stepped pyramid" was adopted, inclined courses were used in both the four-stepped and six-stepped pyramids.[5] No mastabas are known to have been constructed with inclined courses. Presumably, this disposition was an innovation introduced by Imhotep, Djoser's famous architect, to ensure solidity in the newly

---

[1] J. P. Lauer, *La Pyramide à Degrès*, *L'Architecture*, 1936, Tome 1, p. 217, in the series *Fouilles à Saqqara*, Service des Antiquités de l'Egypte.

[2] G. A. Reisner in *Bulletin of the Museum of Fine Arts*, Boston, Dec. 1911, p. 56.

[3] W. M. F. Petrie, *Meidum*, p. 6.

[4] J. P. Lauer, *op. cit.*, p. 216.

[5] J. P. Lauer, *op. cit.*, pp. 17–19.

designed pyramid structure.[6] And here we have a huge central stone edifice, built of independent layers with inclined courses, on a square plan, and surrounded by a great enclosure wall of fine limestone. This leaves little doubt as to the nature of the monument.

Because of the slope of the rock base, it was necessary to build up the surface in places to secure a level platform on which the pyramid could be constructed. The result was that the level of the pyramid is not the same as that of the unfinished northern enclosure wall (the White Wall). The difference in levels is: at the northwest corner of the pyramid, 187 inches, and at the southeast corner, 61 inches.

It might be thought that, since the building had been used as a quarry in later times, it existence was known until a comparatively recent date. Fortunately I was able to satisfy myself that the monument had been undisturbed for at least 3,000 years and probably for longer. Proof of this lay in the large number of later burials which my workmen found during the excavations, and as the earliest of these dated from the Nineteenth Dynasty (1349–1197 B.C.), and as some were found lying undisturbed *above the buried pyramid itself*, it is obvious that the walls we had uncovered had not been seen by human eyes since that remote epoch.

Some lay above the pyramid structure and others in

---

[6] J. P. Lauer, *Études Complémentaires sur les Monuments du Roi Zoser à Saqqara* (le fascicule), p. 25 in the series, *Supplément aux Annales du Service des Antiquités de l'Egypte*, Cahier No. 9.

the enclosure, and the fact that so many burials were concentrated in this area shows that it must have been regarded as a sacred site for more than 2,500 years after the
pyramid was built.

So many of these graves have been found (and more
will almost certainly be discovered) that it is not possible
at this stage to give more than a brief description of them.
When I have had time for fuller examination, I hope to
publish a more detailed account in a later volume.

Perhaps the most interesting burial is that shown in
illustration 10, of a lady called Ka-Nefer-Nefer ("The
Twice-beautiful Ka"). The body was unmummified and
wrapped in a mat of palm reeds. The head and shoulders
were covered with a realistic mask of stuccoed pasteboard
and canvas with gilding and painting, a necklace composed
of beads made of glass colored in imitation of semiprecious stones, together with amulets of green felspar
and glass, and statuettes of alabaster, steatite and wood.
There was also the body of an unknown man wearing a set
of jewelry including finger rings of gold and carnelian,
some of which bear the name of Rameses II. Both these
burials date from the first half of the Nineteenth Dynasty.
These people appear to have belonged to a Libyan tribe
which chose this site as a cemetery.

There were a large number of unmummified burials,
most of which were without jewelry or adornments of any
kind. The mats are of palm ribs, reeds, rushes, or papyrus
stems tied with cords (see illustration 10), and contained
nothing but the bones. Some had pottery jars laid beside

them. Similar "mat-burials" were found by Borchardt at Abusir and by Jacques de Morgan at Dashur, but not in such quantities as on this site. While we were digging out the pyramid and the White Wall, hardly a day passed without our finding these burials, which Borchardt believed to have been of a Libyan tribe, not Egyptians. Others are recorded in the account of the excavations at Sakkara in 1907 and 1908 by Quibell.

So far I have dealt only with the superstructure of the pyramid. I knew that subterranean galleries and chambers must lie underneath, and subsequently I was able to explore some of them, as will be described later. In the meantime it was necessary to learn everything possible about the building itself, and in particular to see if any clues existed which would help us to understand how these mighty monuments were built. A complete pyramid, such as that of Khufu or Menkaure, can tell us little about its internal structure and the methods by which it was built. An incomplete pyramid such as this one might tell us something.

Therefore, before I take up the story of the discovery and exploration of the underground passages, I shall devote a chapter to a brief summary of what is known about pyramid construction during the Third Dynasty, concluding with the information I have been able to glean so far from the new monument.

SIX

The Building of a Pyramid

IT WILL BE RECALLED THAT THE KINGS WHO EVENTUALLY gained control of the whole of Egypt came from the southern part of the country, *i.e.*, Upper Egypt, and that their capital was originally at This, hence the term the "Thisite" kings. Then, at the end of the Second Dynasty (*circa* 2800 B.C.), they established their new capital at Memphis, from which they controlled the entire land. The tombs which they built in Upper Egypt were of a different type from those which we have seen at Sakkara, of which Djoser's pyramid was the finest example.

Professor George Andrew Reisner, in his monumental work, *The Development of the Egyptian Tomb down to the Accession of Cheops,*[1] observes:

> In Upper Egypt up to this time [*i.e.*, end of Dyn. II] the substructures of the royal tombs and the private tombs were c.b. [crude brick] structures built in open pits in the gravel and roofed with wood or c.b. corbel vaults. At Memphis in Dyn. II the type developed was the deep stairway type with rock-cut underground chambers, on a com-

---

[1] Following excerpts reprinted by permission of the Harvard University Press, Cambridge, Mass. Copyright 1936, pp. 153–154.

plex plan in the larger tombs and with one chamber in the smaller. With Dyn. III the capital was definitely moved to Memphis and Memphite types began to dominate the whole country.

The reason for this change was the development of stone cutting at Memphis. As Reisner says:

> The Egyptian craftsmen had mastered the cutting of blocks of limestone to such an extent that they were able to quarry limestone blocks of almost any size and on royal demand to excavate very large pits and trenches (or stairways) in the rock. But it was only for royal buildings that stone was used in any great amount and in these the blocks used were small in relation to those used in Dyn. IV at Giza. The buildings which composed the tomb of Zoser and its enceinte are the earliest we have at present, made of dressed stone. In masonry and in architectural details these buildings present a translation into white limestone (comparatively small blocks) of the older c.b. architecture of Dyn. II.

I have already described briefly, in Chapter Four, the manner of quarrying and shaping the stone. But the methods used by the Ancient Egyptian masons varied according to the type of building under construction, and those of pyramid building are still incompletely understood. Among the best authorities are Somers Clarke and R. Engelbach, whose book, *Ancient Egyptian Masonry*,[2]

---

[2] Oxford University Press, London, 1930.

can be relied upon for hard unspeculative information. Another is I. E. S. Edwards' more up-to-date work, *The Pyramids of Egypt*.[3]

First it must be remembered that a pyramid was a religious monument, and its foundation was accompanied by elaborate rites and ceremonies, the main outlines of which are known.[4] They seem to have been performed by the king himself, with the assistance of priests and priestesses dressed as gods and goddesses.[5] The main parts of the ceremony consisted of:

(1) Pegging out the ground and stretching the cord.
(2) Breaking the surface of the ground.
(3) Sprinkling sand.
(4) Making bricks.
(5) Laying bricks.

The last two ceremonies are interesting: probably they were survivals of the days when tombs were made of mud-brick before stone masonry was used.

During the foundation ceremonies specimens of materials used in the building were buried beneath the foundation. We call these Foundation Deposits. Most of the deposits so far discovered date only from the Middle Kingdom and later, but there is little doubt that similar cere-

---

[3] Pelican Books, London, 1954.
[4] From the solar temple and pyramid complex of Nieussera.
[5] Von Bissing and Kees, "Rathures," 1922, pp. 13–21, *Journal of Egyptian Archaeology*, xx. 183–4. Also reliefs on the Temples of Edfu and Dendera.

monies took place during earlier periods. These objects were sometimes foundation tablets of brick, metal, stone, or wood, usually bearing the name of the king. Beneath the pyramid of Amenemhat the First was found a deposit consisting of an ox skull, broken pottery vases, and six clay bricks, each brick containing a tablet inscribed with the name of the king and his pyramid. This custom has its modern secular parallels. It is not so very far removed from the ceremonial burial of current newspapers and coins beneath the local town hall!

The ground having been consecrated and the appropriate rites performed, the next stage was to construct those parts of the edifice which were to be below the level of the ground. We have already examined, in Chapter Two, the Unfinished Pyramid at Zawiyet-el-Eryan, with its deep pit approached by a sloping ramp and stairway. It is important to distinguish between this "open-trench" construction, as seen at Zawiyet-el-Eryan, and the "tunneled" substructure beneath Djoser's pyramid, and, as we shall see later, beneath the new monument. But in both these structures the sarcophagus chamber, to contain the body of the king, was at the bottom of an open pit which was afterward filled with rubble and masonry. This chamber was usually wholly in the substructure, and was lined with granite brought from Assuan in Upper Egypt. The roofing blocks for the chamber were cut to shape and numbered before being put into position. In Djoser's chamber the markings are still visible.

Next, the sarcophagus, to contain the body, was

dragged over the approach ramp and placed in position. However, this is true only of pyramids built after the time of Djoser. It seems doubtful that Djoser's burial chamber ever contained a coffin. The chamber measured only 9' 10" by 3' 3" by 5' 5" and was entered through a hole in the granite roof, which was sealed by a huge granite plug like the stopper in a bottle (if one can imagine a stopper weighing three and a half tons). In the *The Step Pyramid*, by Firth and Quibell,[6] the former states:

> The comparatively small size of the interior of the sarcophagus chamber . . . shows that it probably never contained an inner wooden coffin and it is unlikely that the pieces of wood composing it could have been introduced through the hole fitted with the granite plug, while the aperture is in fact so small that a body wrapped in linen could only be introduced with a certain amount of difficulty.

Other subterranean galleries were tunneled out beneath the site of the pyramid, usually linked with the entrance corridor (though beneath Djoser's pyramid there were other passages with separate approaches) leading to burial chambers for other members of the royal family,[7] and to magazines or store chambers for funerary furniture and the innumerable stone vessels intended to provide sustenance for the king in the after-life. Some of these

---

[6] C. M. Firth and J. E. Quibell, *The Step Pyramid*, in the series, Excavations of Sakkara, *Service des Antiquités de l'Egypte*, Cairo, 1935, p. 3.
[7] Though these were sometimes added later.

vessels, jars and bowls may have contained food, but others were of a ritual character and probably did not contain anything. To understand the mind of the Ancient Egyptian, it is necessary to realize the powerful part played in his life by magic. It was not always necessary for the dead man to possess the *real* object; sometimes a representation was sufficient, and instead of real food offerings, the food vessels alone would suffice.

It is difficult to estimate the number of such vessels found beneath Djoser's pyramid. Writing of one gallery or magazine, Quibell states:

> This last gallery proves to be, not a tomb, but a magazine or rather two magazines, each some thirty meters [almost 100 feet] long, part of one above the other, separated by only half a meter [about 20 inches] of rock. Both are filled to the roof with stacks of alabaster vases and bowls. The roof has fallen in and crushed most of them to small fragments. *There must be about ninety tons* of weight of them.[8] [Our italics.]

Sometimes this smashing was not accidental, but was done by the men who placed the vessels in the magazines. There is a note in Firth's diary describing galleries which he found beneath three long galleries in the southwest terrace of the pyramid.

> Great quantities of stone vessel fragments were obtained from the southern end of these galleries, but the quantity of these vessels is less than those from the Step

---

[8] C. M. Firth and J. E. Quibell, *The Step Pyramid.*

Pyramid itself. There is every evidence of intentional destruction and scattering.

I mention these, to us, fantastic customs only to emphasize the mental gulf which separates us from the Ancient Egyptians, a gulf which must be bridged if we are to understand the meaning and purpose of their monuments.

Incidentally these beautifully made stone vases (see illustration 22a) provide us with a clue to methods used by the Third Dynasty masons in building a stone monument. Such fine vessels had been made for centuries before Djoser's time, and when, at last, under Imhotep's guidance, the Ancient Egyptians began to build with stone blocks, this inherited skill in stone carving showed clearly in their work.

Great skill in building there certainly is [writes Firth], but it is not the skill which comes from centuries of handling stone *and the realization of the possibilities natural to that material.* Everything is built up solid and then carved like a statue. For example, the vertical grooves or panels in the walls have been laboriously cut out afterwards with the flint borer and copper chisel. There is great waste of labour and material in the dressing and fitting of the small blocks of stone. It is the art of stone cutters who had a long tradition of stone vase making (an industry which had begun to decline by the IIIrd Dynasty), but who were treating stone almost as a plastic material. Just as the stone vessels seek to make more permanent and beautiful the forms of those of clay while creating new forms for themselves, so did those first builders in stone seek to make the forms of mud brick and reed building imperishable (Firth and Quibell, p. 23).

While the subterranean passages were being hollowed out work went ahead above ground to prepare the site of the pyramid itself. Sometimes, as in Djoser's pyramid and the newly discovered one, the foundations were laid on the solid rock, after preliminary leveling. At other times it was necessary to build a level platform of rubble. Leveling was probably done by the method described in Chapter Four, *i.e.*, linking up the square base area, flooding it, and then marking the water level on the banks. In the case of the new pyramid a considerable amount of leveling had been done, as I was able to establish by means of a theodolite.

Meanwhile the architect would have drawn up a plan, giving the dimensions worked out in cubits, and the angle of slope. Engelbach notes:

> In the pyramids of Snofru at Medum and of Khufu at Giza the proportions are such that, if a circle be imagined whose circumference is equal to the perimeter of the base of the pyramid, the radius of that circle will be its height. This gives an angle of 51° 51' for the angle of the casing (or tangent—1. $^{14}/_{11}$).[9]

Mathematical problems connected with pyramids occur in two papyri, one known as the Rhind Mathematical

---

[9] S. Clarke and R. Engelbach, *Ancient Egyptian Masonry*, Oxford University Press, 1930.

The Building of a Pyramid

Papyrus and the other the Moscow Papyrus. Here is one from the Rhind Papyrus:

Problem: Pyramid 140 cubits long and 5 palms 1 finger in its batter [slope].
What is its vertical height?

Solution: Divide 1 cubit by twice the batter, which amounts to 10 palms 2 fingers [10½ palms].
Reckon with 10½ to find 7, for 7 palms 1 cubit.
Two-thirds of 10½ is 7.
Reckon with 140, for this is the length of the side.
Make ⅔ of 140, namely 93⅓.
This is the vertical height thereof.

The Egyptians had only one method of expressing the slope angle: to state it in terms of a vertical rise of 1 cubit on a horizontal base of so many palms and fingers. They were unaware of any other means of expressing angles.

Finally the site would be carefully surveyed to establish the four cardinal points. The Ancient Egyptians did not possess the compass, yet they achieved an accuracy of orientation which is truly astonishing. In the Great Pyramid, for example, a building measuring over 750 feet square, the errors in the four sides are the following fractions of *one degree:*

North side .	.	2' 28" south of west.
South side .	.	1' 57" south of west.
East side .	.	5' 30" west of north.
West side .	.	2' 30" west of north.

THE LOST PYRAMID

The methods which the Egyptians used to achieve this amazing degree of precision are not fully known— most probably by sighting on a star in the northern heavens and bisecting the angle formed by its rising position, the position from which the observation was made, and the setting position. This would give true north, after which the other cardinal points could easily be established.

In one brief chapter there is only space to give the barest outline of pyramid construction, but something must be said concerning the organization of labor, the sequence of operations, and the method of building, in so far as this is known. I shall not speculate on the many theories which have been put forward throughout the ages to account for the way in which the huge megalithic blocks of later pyramids were hauled into position, except to say that there is no evidence whatsoever to support the belief that the Ancient Egyptians possessed any mechanical apparatus more complicated than the lever, the roller and the inclined plane. There is not even any evidence to show that they possessed the pulley. Engelbach and other authorities believe that the blocks were hauled up ramps by sheer man power, slid into position on a bed of liquid mortar (which thus acted as a lubricant) and finally shaped *in situ*. No representation of a pulley and tackle exists on any Egyptian painting or relief, nor are there evidences on the blocks of marks left by the tongs or "lewises" which would almost certainly have shown had they been used. Even the yards of Egyptian ships were pushed up from below, not hauled up. On the other hand, the granite plug sealing the burial chamber in the southern tomb of Djoser, to which I shall refer later, was undoubtedly raised and lowered by a rope that passed over a beam which is still in position. But that was *inside* the building. There is no evidence that the Egyptians had portable lifting tackle which could be used externally.

However, this problem would not occur in the pyramids of the Third Dynasty, since the stones were of comparatively small size and could be carried comfortably by two men.

I have explained in Chapter Four how the stone was quarried and the workmen organized in crews and gangs. A vast and complex administrative system must have existed to make possible the quarrying of the blocks, their transport across the river (in the case of the fine limestone for the outer facing), and the erection of the monument itself, with an army of scribes to keep check, to mark the blocks where necessary, and to arrange for the housing and feeding of the great numbers of builders, quarriers, craftsmen, and others who were employed on these monuments. Sometimes we find relics of these ancient workmen: carrying-baskets just like those used today, flint borers and scrapers, copper tools, fragments of rope. When the cave-like quarries of Tura were cleared, quantities of thick, well-made rope were found, left there thousands of years ago by the Ancient Egyptian workmen. To facilitate the carrying of the Tura-quarried limestone from the riverside to the pyramid, a causeway was built; examples of these still remain at Giza, Sakkara, Dashur, Abusir and other places.

THE LOST PYRAMID

By comparison with their masters, the anonymous Egyptian workmen who built these great monuments have left hardly any memorials, which makes it very difficult for us to reconstruct their lives with any authenticity. We know about the tools they used, and something of their working methods. We know how they were organized into gangs. What else do we know?

Something about their living quarters: at Medinet Habu, near Luxor, archaeologists discovered extensive remains of long barracklike buildings in which were housed the workmen engaged on making the Eighteenth and Nineteenth Dynasty tombs in the Theban Necropolis. Near the Great Pyramid at Giza, Petrie, and later Reisner, found similar foundations of barrack buildings. Petrie describes another of these towns, at Kahun, built in the Twelfth Dynasty.

> The houses may be of any size, from four rooms to six, and each street contains a uniform size of house. The streets vary in length; one is 62 feet long for two houses, others are 230 feet long for eight or nine houses. . . . The streets vary from 11 to 15 feet wide. They had a channel down the middle for a drain, like the old English kennel. There was no separate footway, because there were no vehicles in such a town.

Petrie says that the simple houses had an open court opposite the entrance, a common room on one side, and the store rooms on the other, with a stairway up to the roof. The larger type had four rooms opening off an open court and five others dependent on the outer rooms.

The doors of these houses were of wood, with wooden sills and a lintel built into the wall; when the pivot holes wore down the owners put some leather under the pivot, usually a bit of worn-out sandal.

Allowing for the difference of climate and custom, such artisans' dwellings were probably superior to the "back to back" workers' dwellings in the industrial north of England, and to some of the working-class houses of industrial America.

When we come to discuss methods of payment, we have no standards by which we can compare them with those of the modern world. In ancient Egypt, especially in the early period, payment was made in kind. Leonard Cottrell, in his book, *Life under the Pharaohs*, makes the following comment on this:

> To us, with our elaborate banking and currency systems, such an arrangement seems primitive, yet the Ancient Egyptians did not find it inconvenient. They held markets, paid salaries, lent on interest and collected taxes without a coin changing hands.

The superior class of artisan would appear to have enjoyed reasonably comfortable accommodation for himself and his family, but the bulk of the unskilled labor, which was provided by land workers rendered idle by the inundation, probably lived in rough shelters. But they were assured of being fed.

The question which remains to be answered is: "How

were the pyramids actually assembled?" The difficulty in answering this question is that there is no pictorial or written evidence from Ancient Egyptian times. Many ingenious theories have been advanced, some of them fantastic. Herodotus, "The Father of History," who visited Egypt in the fifth century B.C., was given a puzzling explanation, which is worth quoting. In Book II, Cap. 125, the Greek historian states:

> This [the Great] pyramid was built thus: in the form of steps. . . . When they had first built it in this manner, they raised the remaining stones by machines made of short pieces of wood; having lifted them from the ground to the first range of steps, when the stone arrived there, it was put on another machine that stood ready on the first range, and from this it was drawn to the second range on another machine; for the machines were equal in number to the range of steps (or they removed the machine, which was only one, and portable, to each range in succession, whenever they wished to raise the stone higher, or I should relate in both ways, as it is related). The highest parts of it, therefore, were the first finished, and afterwards they completed the parts next following; but last of all they finished the parts on the ground and that were lowest.

He was referring, of course, to the Great Pyramid at Giza, the blocks of which weigh many tons, unlike the Pyramid of Djoser and the new pyramid, which are built of much smaller blocks that could be lifted without mechanical aid. Even so, it is extremely doubtful if the "short

1. The author,
M. Zakaria Goneim.

2. The Step Pyramid
of King Djoser: 2,800 B.C.

3. Reconstruction of entrance to outer enclosure of Djoser's Pyramid.

4. The work begins on the Lost Pyramid. In the distance are the pyramids of Sno at Dashur.

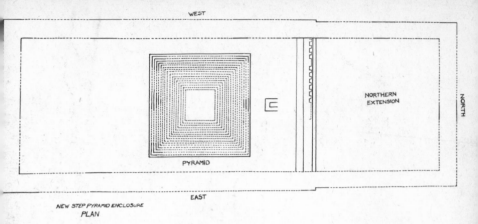

WEST

NORTHERN
EXTENSION

NORTH

PYRAMID

EAST

NEW STEP PYRAMID ENCLOSURE
PLAN

5. A preliminary plan of the Lost Pyramid and its enclosure.

The White Wall of the Lost Pyramid partially uncovered.

7. The White Wall fully uncovered.

8. *Above*, workmen's drawings on one of the bastions of the White Wall. 9. *Left*, interior view of the ancient Egyptian quarries at Maesara in the Eastern cliffs of the Nile. Notice the pillars which have been left to support the roof. 10. *Below*, the "mat" burial of a Libyan lady, Ka Nefer-Nefer. The covering is palm mesh.

11. The southeast corner of the pyramid uncovered, showing the first "step."

The original construction ramp of rubble used in building the pyramid.

The search for the entrance gallery to the north of the remains of the Mortuary Temple.

14. Excavating the approach to the entrance gallery.

15. *Left*, entrance approach fully e[x]vated. 16. *Above*, entrance doorway of pyramid substructure with the blockag[e] position.

17. View from the interior with part of the blocking wall removed.

18. Semi-circular arch 11 meters from the entrance showing rubble forming second blockage.

View from interior corridor, looking upward through the cleared shaft.

20. The sarcophagus chamber as found, looking south. Note the funeral wreath
top.

21. Alabaster sarcophagus showing sliding panel at north end, with wreath in position.

a. An assortment of v
and urns.

b. A bracelet of gold beads with gold spacers.

c. The remains of sacrificed animals, at bottom of pit.

22. Some of the objects found in the Lost Pyramid.

. M. Zakaria Goneim at the entrance of the pyramid. At his right is Hussein Ibrahim, at his left is Hofni Ibrahim.

24. The open sarcophagus. The sliding panel weighed 500 lbs.

pieces of wood" were anything more complicated than levers. Some scholars have drawn attention to model "rockers" found in foundation deposits of the New Kingdom. These consist of two pieces of wood curved at the base like the rockers of a rocking chair and joined by wooden spindles. The suggestion is that the blocks were "rocked" up the side of the pyramid step by step, and laid. But as Clarke and Engelbach point out: [10]

Let it be assumed that there were rockers, in unending numbers, strong enough to support blocks up to 10 tons in weight and that the blocks were rocked up step by step and laid. When the top was reached, the appearance of the monument would be very much like that of the Giza pyramids today. In the putting on of the facing two possibilities present themselves: either the top casing-blocks were also rocked up and the lower courses in some mysterious manner *slipped in below them*, which is a mechanical impossibility, or the appearance of the casing-blocks, before their faces were dressed, was also that of a series of steps, for by no other means could they also be rocked up. This is directly contradicted by the appearance of the unfinished casing-blocks in the Third Pyramid, and also by all other known examples of unfinished masonry.

Another theory is that the "accretion faces"—the independent skins of masonry leaning on a central nucleus —played an essential part in the process of building; that

[10] S. Clarke and R. Engelbach, *Ancient Egyptian Masonry*, Oxford University Press, 1930, p. 121.

the inner core was built first, then the inner accretion wall to its full height, after which the builders would start again from the base and erect the next accretion wall, and so on until the building was complete.

The principal argument against this theory is that, as the Ancient Egyptians did not possess lifting tackle, the blocks would have to be handled *from the front*. The only way in which the huge blocks used in the later pyramids could have been hauled into position was by means of ramps built against the side of the structure. We know that this system was used in later times, as a scene of the New Kingdom depicts a wall being built in this way; also until fairly recently one could still see such a ramp built against one of the pylons in the Temple of Karnak.[11] There are also remains of such ramps at the Pyramid of Amenemhat I at Lisht and at the Pyramid of Medum.

Now, if we are to accept the belief that each of the accretion walls was built to its full height before the next was begun, we would have to assume that after each wall was completed the huge mud-brick ramp would be moved back to make room for the building of the next skin of masonry, which would involve an enormous waste of labor; and we know that the Egyptians were very efficient organizers of labor. The tendency now is to regard these accretion walls as being intended only *to give stability to the structure*, and to believe that, in fact, they were all built simultaneously.

---

[11] S. Clarke and R. Engelbach, *op. cit.*, Fig. 87.

The Building of a Pyramid

Supporters of this theory think that the sequence of construction was as follows. The foundation platform having been made, the builders would lay the first courses of masonry. Against one side of the pyramid they would then build a supply ramp up which the stones were hauled on sledges.

As the pyramid rose in height, so the ramp was increased both in height and in length; simultaneously the top surface would become progressively narrower to correspond with the constantly diminishing breadth of the pyramid face. If the angle of incline of the pyramid were 52°, the two side faces of the ramp would also slope at an angle of 52°, so that any risk of "land-slides" would be eliminated. The three sides of the pyramid which were not covered by the supply ramp would have foot-hold embankments of sufficient width at the top to allow for the passage of men and building material, but, since they were not required for raising the stones from the ground their gradient on the exposed outer surface could be as steep as would be compatible with firmness. Wooden baulks, some of which were actually found *in situ* by the American excavators at Lisht, would be placed on the top surface of both the supply ramp and the foot-hold embankments in order to provide a firm roadway for the passage of sledges bearing the stone blocks.

The above-quoted passage, from Mr. I. E. S. Edwards' excellent book, *The Pyramids of Egypt*, indicates the current trend of thought on pyramid building. Although he is writing mainly on the later pyramids built of megalithic blocks, there is no reason to suppose that the same method was not used in the construction of the earlier pyramids, such as Djoser's monument and that which I have discovered.

To return again to the new pyramid: during the course of my excavations in the season of 1953–54, I found evidence which appears to confirm the above theory, although full confirmation can only be made after further investigation of the area surrounding the pyramid. On four sides of the structure I found traces of what are almost certainly construction embankments—the "foot-hold embankments" described above, which were intended to give the workmen access to the higher portions of the monument. They are formed of *tafl* (chips of soft clay) from the underground galleries. An interesting fact which I noted is that the top of these embankments is higher than the present level of the pyramid, suggesting that it was originally built up to a higher level than the present one, and that the upper courses have been removed during quarrying operations.

Also, on the west side of the structure, nearest the quarry, we found part of the original construction ramp up which the stones were hauled. This ramp and the foothold embankments can be clearly seen in illustration 12. Had the pyramid been completed, the ramp and embankments would gradually have been removed as the casing-stones were put on, an operation which I shall describe in a later chapter summing up my conclusions. It is still early to prophesy, but one fact seems certain: that we have here the first example of a pyramid actually under construction, perhaps providing an opportunity of solving problems which have puzzled generations of archaeologists.

SEVEN

The Search for the Entrance Gallery

THE WORK I HAVE DESCRIBED TOOK US UP TO THE FIRST
week of January, 1954. The rest of that month was spent
in trying to locate the hidden entrance to the substructure.
As I have stated, pyramids were always accurately ori-
entated to the four cardinal points, and in those of the
Third, Fourth, Fifth and Sixth Dynasties the entrances
were always on the central axis of the north side.

The reasons for this cannot be understood without
some knowledge of the king's fate after death.

When the king died, he was believed to become one
with Osiris, the god of the dead. The tomb confines the
king's body, but the gates of the earth open when Anubis,
the god of the necropolis, calls the king. And the latter's
soul goes forth to heaven after passing through the sacred
region of Abydos, where his ancestors were buried.

In heaven he is received by the spirits of his ancestors
who transform him to a blessed and exalted spirit. Thus
he awakens to eternal life. Then he is introduced into
the hereafter by the Sun-god, Re, who enthrones him as

King of the Dead. He moves in heaven, joining the sun in its circuit.

Thou descendest with him [the Sun-god]

Thou risest and openest the way through
the bones of Shu [the god of the air].

Thou risest and settest; thou risest up with Re . . .
Thou risest and settest; . . . sinking down in
the dusk with the Evening Boat of the Sun.[1]

Thou risest and settest; thou risest up with
Isis, ascending with the Morning Boat of the Sun.
                    (From texts in the Pyramid of Unis)

He also moves with the stars on "the beautiful roads of heaven." He is identified with one of the circumpolar stars. In this capacity he circles round the pole in the northern part of the sky. To enable him to attain that point it was essential that the entrance to his pyramid should be on the northern side.[2]

The original entrance to Djoser's pyramid also lies on the north side, but at some distance from the monument.

First I had to determine if there was an entrance at

---

[1] The two so-called Solar Boats in which the sun was supposed to perform his night journey from west to east and his day journey from east to west respectively. The first was called "the Bark of the Dusk," and the second, "the Bark of the Dawn."

[2] H. Frankfort, *Kingship and the Gods*, Chicago, 1948, pp. 111–118.

all—though I had little doubt of this, since I was sure that no superstructure would have been built without beginning the substructure. It should be to the north, and on the central axis, I knew, but at what point? I first uncovered the central part of the north side of the pyramid, then excavated the area immediately to the north of it. Soon I found what appeared to be the remains of a mortuary temple. I should mention at this point that Egyptian pyramids usually had two temples, one on the boundary of the desert and the cultivated valley, and the other near the pyramid itself. These were joined by the stone causeway already described, originally built to facilitate the transport of stone, and later apparently used for religious purposes.

Few examples of the lower temples remain, and their purpose is uncertain, but possibly they were used for the ritual washing of the king's body before embalmment, and perhaps for the embalming ceremony itself. They contained storerooms, cult-rooms, and sometimes there are basins and channels, perhaps connected with the funeral rites. The best-preserved Lower or "Valley" Temple is that of Chephren at Giza. No traces of a valley temple of Djoser exist.

The Upper or Mortuary Temple stood near the pyramid itself. That of Djoser is on the north side, but from the time of Snofru onward they were normally sited on the east side. Again the functions of these buildings are incompletely known, but they seem to have been used for offerings, presented in an offering shrine. Here also the priests may have performed the ceremony of "Opening of the Mouth," by which the mummy and the statues of the king were ritually given life.

This ceremony was based on a complicated series of rituals which were essentially magical in character. The officiant in that ceremony was the *sem* priest who represented Horus, the son of Osiris. As the deceased king impersonated Osiris, this priest was the king's son, or if not his son, usually his successor, whether he happened to be his real son or not. Clad in a panther's skin, the officiant, directed by the lector-priest, would give back to the dead king the use of his organs by touching the face of his mummy with various magical instruments, chiefly the "adze" (or the foreleg of a calf which was slain on this occasion) and the "chisel." [3] The mouth and the eyes were then anointed with seven sacred oils or unguents. Thus the dead monarch would be enabled to partake of the food and drink which were considered necessary for his survival, and to enjoy the use of all vital functions in the hereafter. Then the mummy had to undergo the ceremonial "toilet." This toilet was based upon the daily lustrations which Re, the Sun-god, was supposed to perform before he began his journey across the sky.

---

[3] The adze and the foreleg were the earthly substitutes for a heavenly prototype, our Great Bear or Plough, the most conspicuous of the northern constellations. This group of stars appears in the ancient Egyptian sky maps in the form of a carpenter's adze (such as was used in Egypt) and later as the foreleg of an ox. In the Pyramid Texts, the adze is described as an instrument of iron "which opened the mouth of the gods . . . with that wherewith he (Horus) opened the mouth of Osiris, with the *iron* which came forth from the *Great Bear.*" The "chisel" must have been of similar character also. For the origin of this idea and its development, see the remarkable essay: *A Pair of Constellations*, published by G. A. Wainwright in *Studies Presented to F. Le. Griffith*, Egypt Exploration Society, London, 1932, pp. 373–383.

That elaborate ceremony was begun by the purification of the mummy with holy water, to make it a pure abode for the ka,[4] and the burning of incense, and ended with a sacred meal for the revivified king as well as for the mourners. After the meal, acts of mourning were performed, which were really ceremonies of farewell. Finally the mummy was put into its appointed place in the tomb.

Besides the offering shrines the mortuary temple also contained storerooms, antechambers, and groups of statues. Some of the finest examples of Egyptian statuary have been found in these pyramid temples.

The mortuary temple of Djoser was built over the entrance to his pyramid, so when I uncovered buildings on the north side of the newly found structure which appeared to be the remains of a mortuary building, I naturally sought for the entrance there, but without result. Then I shifted the work still farther to the north, but still on the central axis of the pyramid, at a point where I had noticed a peculiar concavity in the sand (see illustration 13). It was in the form of a concave crescent, and suggested that there might be a hollow underneath. There was also another significant clue. All around the pyramid was a square embankment resulting from the quarrying of the pyramid structure, and in the middle of this embankment was a breach. This encouraged me to excavate the area

---

[4] Since the word "ka" will be found frequently in this story, particularly in the latter part, a word of explanation may be helpful. Steindorff equates this term with the English "guardian spirit," Erman calls it "vital power," and Maspero a "double." The "ka" was born at the same time as the individual; it was imperishable in the after-life, it was a protective genius.

completely, and on February 2, 1954, at a distance of about 75 feet from the north side of the pyramid, my workmen struck the edge of the walls of the outer approach to the substructure, which proved to be a long, open, rock-cut trench enclosed at the top by massive supporting walls.

My workmen and I were intensely excited. As we dug down into the sand and more and more of the trench became visible, it was clear that we were nearing the entrance to the pyramid substructure. The question which worried us was: "Would the entrance be found intact, or had tomb robbers entered the pyramid before us?" This is a problem which occupies the minds of all Egyptian archaeologists. People who are not familiar with this work sometimes regard our efforts as a kind of sacrilege. Alas, the truth is that the Ancient Egyptians themselves were far more efficient in the art of tomb robbing than the modern, scientific archaeologist, and far more ruthless. Read the record of Egyptian excavations over the past century, and you will find again and again the melancholy phrase "but the tomb was found to have been robbed in antiquity."

Of all the tombs of the Pharaohs in the Royal Valley at Luxor, only one, that of Tutankhamen, was found almost intact, and even that had been partially robbed, though fortunately the plunderers seem to have been interrupted before they could complete their task. Of the pyramids, there is not one which was not ransacked thousands of years ago. The reason is simple. The custom of burying the kings in coffins of gold, adorned with golden ornaments and surrounded by valuable funerary furniture, was too much of a temptation to those who followed.

> There must have been a time [writes Baikie] [5] when more wealth, both in sheer bullion and in artistic craftsmanship, was stored away . . . than in any other spot in the world; but it is highly improbable that it lasted for very long, or, indeed, that even all the treasures of a single Dynasty remained intact at its close, or for more than a few years after. . . . Scheme after scheme failed in its turn; the gigantic pyramids of the Old Kingdom, the elaborate puzzle-passages of the modest pyramids of the Middle Kingdom, alike proved powerless against the hereditary skill of the native Egyptian tomb-robber.

They were brave and desperate men. Leonard Cottrell vividly describes the terrors which had to be overcome by those daring enough to enter the burial chamber of the king.

> Anyone who has visited the sepulchral chambers of the Egyptian kings will remember the awe with which they strike even the least sensitive modern traveller. Imagine, then, the feelings of Amenpfer and his seven companions,[6] fearing the terrible punishment which awaited them if they were caught, but fearing even more the wrath of the king whose tomb they were violating. For to them he was a god. In the flickering light of their torches they would see, on the wall of the burial hall, the carved and painted

---

[5] *Egyptian Antiquities of the Nile Valley*, p. 466.
[6] Theban tomb robbers, the record of whose trial survives.

figures of the denizens of the Underworld, and of the dread gods who were now the companions and protectors of the king. Perhaps some would hesitate, afraid, until greed and desperation drove them on, and the bolder spirits rallied the faint-hearted. Then . . . the ringing blows of the hammers on copper, the splitting open of the sarcophagus, the breaking of the triple coffins, and the tearing of the funeral wrappings. Finally flames and smoke from the burning mummies blackening the sacred inscriptions as the thieves struggled back through their tunnel, clutching the gold and silver ornaments which had adorned the royal bodies. . . .[7]

Had our pyramid witnessed such a scene? As we dug down to the bottom of the trench, impatient to find the entrance, we wondered. We found the approach blocked at intervals with thick masonry and the gaps filled up with loose stones. It contained an incline sloping down from the north and leading to a doorway 6′ 2″ wide and 7′ 8″ high, cut in the living rock. To our extreme relief we found that the doorway was intact, sealed with masonry.

The block of the door was built in two parts which entirely filled it, and, as we discovered later, a considerable part of the inner corridor to which it gave access. The left side of the blockage was made of regular masonry, whereas the right section was roughly built. The fact that the door block was found absolutely intact seemed to indicate that the owner of the unfinished step pyramid had

---

[7] Leonard Cottrell, *The Lost Pharaohs*, London, 1950.

been buried in the substructure. I also formed a theory, subsequently modified, to account for the double blockage. "We may infer," I wrote at the time, "that the left side of the doorway, as well as that of the first part of the inner corridor, had been blocked before the owner died, and the right side left free to serve as a passageway for the introduction of the mummy on the day of burial. Eventually this was closed in its turn after burial."

We opened the pyramid on March 9, 1954, in the presence of the then Minister of Education, Dr. Abbas Ammar; the Director-General of the Department of Antiquities, Dr. Mustapha Amer; and other officials. There were also many representatives of the Egyptian and foreign press, including correspondents from the Near East, Europe, America, and even from Argentina and Brazil. There were many photographers, and representatives of American and European broadcasting companies with their tape recorders. So must the modern archaeologist work!

The Minister himself broke open the blockage with an axe. Afterwards Hofni, Hussein, and others of my workmen enlarged the hole and pulled down the upper half of the masonry on the right-hand side. One by one we scrambled in over the stones, ducking our heads to avoid the rock roof. When we had clambered over the blockage, we jumped down into the open corridor beyond. We found ourselves in a high gallery cut out of the living rock and descending steeply into the earth. Our workmen brought portable acetylene lamps, and with the aid of these we were able to penetrate for a distance of some 60 feet. The Minister and the officials went forward with long strides, eager to discover the pyramid's secret. And then, suddenly, we were all brought to a halt. A mass of rubble filled the corridor from floor to ceiling, blocking all further progress for the time being.

Photographs were taken, and the party scrambled back over the blocking stones into the sunlight again. Later I went back and made a careful, systematic examination of the corridor as far as I could penetrate.

The first part descended for 37′ 1″, to a rock-cut archway, 6′ 2″ wide, 3′ 5½″ deep, and 13′ 1½″ high, which is probably unique in early Egyptian architecture (see illustrations 17 and 18). This first part of the corridor is 6′ 8″ wide, and has a very high, flat ceiling. Past the archway the descending passage continues for 20 feet, 4 inches at the same slope; it grows a little wider, and the ceiling inclines downward and is curved. The end of this part of the corridor, I discovered, is exactly in line with the north side of the pyramid structure above.

Here the passage widens to a breadth of 7′ 2½″, and the slope becomes steeper. Traces on the walls of the corridor indicate that they were originally coated with plaster. A few yards farther on the corridor was blocked by rubble. With my workmen I carefully examined the roof and found that there was a square hole through which the rubble had fallen. I at once gave orders to stop work on the corridor, and we began to search in the superstructure of the pyramid to find the cause of this occurrence. And on March eleventh we found a hole which led to a vertical shaft sunk in the rock, penetrating to the entrance corridor of the pyramid.

The shaft is square in section, 8' 10", and is cut partly in the masonry of the superstructure and partly in the rock beneath. My first problem was to discover if it was contemporary with the pyramid or of a later date. At first it seemed that the latter supposition was correct, and my heart sank, since this would indicate that the pyramid had been known in later times and probably robbed. In the hole at the top of the shaft, which was blocked with large rough stones, we found a large deposit of animal bones. There were several cubic yards of bones and horns of oxen, rams, goats, gazelles, dogs and other animals, buried in a pit which had been dug in the filling at the mouth of the shaft. These remains had been put in in layers, and some of them were wrapped in linen. Between each layer of bones was a layer of fine sand. Many horns showed signs of having been cut with a saw, and some had marks engraved on them. All the rams' horns were of the species *Ovis platyra ægyptiaca*. Some tile amulets and wooden animal figures were found with the remains.

Sixty-two demotic papyri, several of which are fairly large sheets, were found in the bottom layer. These papyri date from the Saitic period (*circa* 600 B.C.) ; some of them bear the name of Ahmose II. The purpose and history of these deposits are still uncertain. However, the fact that they were found in that place does not necessarily denote that they had anything to do with the pyramid, as some of the papyri contain lists of objects received by the Necropolis of Sakkara, and the other objects may have been the remains of sacred animals which died at Memphis and were collected by some religious society or pious personage. Then they were mummified and buried in this cemetery.

In Egypt, the cult of the sacred animal goes back to the most ancient times. Down to the first Persian Conquest (525 B.C.) animals had not been sacred as a species. Rather, priests would select one animal "to be a place of manifestation of a god," in the same manner as they would fashion a statue to serve as a material medium for the appearance of the divinity in the temple. Nearing the twilight of her ancient history, the country gradually degenerated by contact with younger civilizations. By reacting against them, Egypt exaggerated the trends of her own civilization, and instead of venerating a few animals, the Egyptians worshiped entire species. Dozens of such cemeteries, at Sakkara and elsewhere, have yielded enormous numbers of remains of sacred animals.

I thought at first that those who had buried the sacred animals might have penetrated the vertical shaft and found the entrance corridor to which it was connected. But further examination convinced me that this was not so. The mouth of the shaft opens in the pyramid structure at a distance of 23′ south of the north side of the central axis. As a result of quarry work in later times, the surrounding area was transformed into an enormous cavity which gradually filled up with debris and sand. But when I dug farther down the square shaft I found it partially filled with heavy stones, which were undisturbed, and long vertical marks left by these falling stones remained on the rock walls of the shaft. Whoever made the hole for the burial of the sacred animals had merely dug down a short distance into the shaft.

I concluded that the original builders had sunk a shaft or square section down to the sloping corridor. This they had filled with heavy stones thrown down from above. About it they had probably built some kind of construction to hide the shaft, which was under the pyramid superstructure itself. During the Saitic Period (Twenty-sixth Dynasty) those who buried the animals had found the shaft and dug a shallow pit at the top. They may have intended to dig right down to the bottom, but did not.

Shafts of this kind are sometimes found in tombs of the Third Dynasty. In certain examples of these tombs they were used for portcullis blockings.[8] The best parallel is the tomb of Sa-nakht at Bet Khallaf.[9] In other examples they were sunk in order to gain greater depth for chambers. For instance, this occurs in the tomb of Hesy-Re at Sakkara.[10] Hesy-Re was a great personage, an overseer of the royal scribes at the time of Djoser. In his tomb were found the famous wooden panels, now in the Cairo Museum, which reveal the vigorous type of man who helped Djoser to create his new monarchy.

---

[8] In later pyramids the passages were closed at intervals by blocks of granite which slid in grooves like a portcullis.

[9] G. A. Reisner, *The Development of the Egyptian Tomb down to the Accession of Cheops*, p. 186.

[10] See plan, Plate L, in J. E. Quibell, *The Tomb of Hesy* (*Service des Antiquités*, Excavations at Sakkara, 1911–12).

It is possible, however, that this shaft was also devised for ventilation in the course of the work.

At the bottom of the shaft the corridor was obstructed by large blocks of stone which had been deliberately thrown down from the mouth by the builders of the pyramid. A huge blockage, more than 15 feet thick, was thus formed, and it was this which had barred our passage when we first entered the pyramid. My first task, therefore, was to clear this shaft from the top, in order to gain access to the corridor. It was at this stage of the work that, unhappily, there was a fatal accident in which one of my men was killed.

I was working in the southwestern angle of the great enclosure at the time, when I heard terrible shouting from the direction of the pyramid. I went rapidly to the spot. At the top of the vertical shaft I found a scene of consternation and terror. My men were gathered around the brink of the dark pit in a state of great agitation. A ladder ran down the side of the shaft. The men had been engaged in hauling out the heavy stones which blocked the shaft, and had gone down to a depth of some 15 feet. I looked down and saw that in the bottom of the half-cleared pit was a yawning hole. During the clearing of the shaft some of the loose stone blockage had given way, precipitating several of the workmen into the corridor below.

We rushed back to the pyramid entrance, scrambled over the half-opened blocking wall and hurried to the base of the shaft. A heavy fall of sand and rock had buried the workmen. An alarm was sent out for an ambulance and firemen with ladders. Meanwhile my workmen and I struggled to remove the sand and rock and to rescue our comrades. We worked feverishly, hauling at the heavy stones, and at last the men were freed. Two had sustained slight injuries, but, alas, the third had been suffocated.

Meanwhile the news had spread to the villages of Sakkara, Abusir, and other nearby villages, and men and women came hurrying to the spot. It was getting dark, and in the gathering dusk I found several hundred people assembled around the top of the shaft, the women uttering wailing cries. I tried to calm their fears, but it was no use. As night descended cars began to arrive from Cairo. The press had heard of the disaster, and there were rumors that the pyramid had entirely collapsed, burying eighty men. The lights of the cars' headlamps lit up the desert and threw into shadow the pit in which the tragedy had occurred. It was a night I shall never forget.

An inquiry was held, and for two weeks all work stopped. No local workmen would come near the pyramid. They were afraid of it; some said that the king who built it was angry, and that the pyramid was evil, that it had a power to swallow and engulf them. This may sound superstitious to readers who have not worked in these monuments, but I can well understand it. I have felt afraid myself and am not ashamed to admit it.

I tried to calm the fears of the men, telling them that we were only trying to make this unknown king known, just as the Pharaoh Tutankhamen, who had been known only to a handful of scholars, became famous all over the world when Lord Carnarvon and Howard Carter discovered his tomb just thirty years ago. Finally the men began to drift back, and after fourteen days we were able once again to attack the pyramid.

EIGHT

Into the Depths

A GREAT DEAL OF ROMANTIC NONSENSE HAS BEEN WRITTEN about the excavation of Ancient Egyptian tombs, and perhaps in reaction against this some archaeologists "lean over backward" in order to be coldly scientific, as if emotion was in some way unscholarly. Yet some of the greatest archaeologists have admitted to having been moved by their discoveries, and in the pages of such men as Petrie, Reisner, Firth and Quibell one can find passages of vivid descriptive writing, side by side with careful, and, to the non-specialist, tedious descriptions of fragments of pottery and other minutiae of interest only to the scholar.

If I were to attempt to write in a detached way, I would not be true to myself. Therefore I shall admit frankly that when, a fortnight after the accident, I reassembled my men and recommenced the work of clearing the entrance corridor, I was strangely uneasy. It is difficult to describe this feeling. It was certainly not fear of anything physical, such as the collapse of a roof or a fall of rock; it was something much less tangible, a mixture of awe, curiosity and uncertainty. No one who has not crawled along the galleries beneath a pyramid, and experienced the silence and darkness, can fully appreciate the sensation which at times overwhelms one. It may sound fantastic, but I felt that the pyramid had a personality and that this personality was that of the king for whom it was built and which still lingered within it. I know that my workmen, some of whom have spent their whole lives in such work, often experience this feeling. You crawl along some dark corridor on hands and knees, past falls of rock; the light of the lamp gleams on minute crystals in the stratified walls; beyond, the corridor disappears into the blackness. You turn corners, feeling your way with your hands; the workmen have been left behind, and suddenly you realize you are alone in a place which has not heard a footfall for nearly fifty centuries. Above you is more than 100 feet of solid rock, and above that again rests the bulk of the pyramid. No one with imagination can have such an experience and not be profoundly stirred.

We began by completing the clearance of the thick wall of rubble which lay at the foot of the shaft. We found that the lowermost parts of this shaft, together with a considerable portion of the roof of the corridor, had fallen down, perhaps because of earthquakes in remote times or natural decay, for much of the rock was of bad quality. When the Ancient Egyptians sank such shafts and galleries, they often went down to a considerable depth, not only for security but in order to find a stratum of good rock from which they could hew the burial chamber.

There were numerous long cracks across the ceiling and down the sides of the passage, and these called for a great deal of consolidation work with masonry and timber before we dared to proceed farther down the corridor. When the mass of stones at the foot of the shaft had been removed, we realized that the bottom layer stood on a thick bed of soft clay which stretched over one yard beyond the blockage on the north side. Underneath this clay we found hundreds of stone vessels of many kinds, similar to those found in the subterranean galleries of Djoser's pyramid. There were hundreds of bowls, of mottled black and white porphyritic rock, cups and dishes of alabaster. They had been placed in layers. The bowls were not large, but generally heavy and only slightly hollowed out. Evidently they had been made for funerary purposes only. (See illustration 22a) . Almost all of them had small unperforated handles. Some of the vessels were broken. As these were found only in the uppermost layer, it seems that the breakage was caused by the crushing weight of the blocking stones flung down the vertical shaft.

But a magnificent surprise find awaited us. When we had cleared the floor of the passage and were examining the clay stratum beneath, one of my men detected the gleam of gold at a spot near the east wall of the corridor. I knelt down and, carefully clearing away the clay, recovered twenty-one golden bracelets and armlets, and a hollow, sickle-shaped gold wand, the core of which had been of wood, now perished. But the gem of the collection was a small box for cosmetics made of embossed gold in the shape of a bivalve shell, of the species known as the *Coquille St. Jacques*. It is composed of two identical concave leaves fastened together with rivets, and is of exquisite workmanship. At the top of the lid is a loop by means of which the box was opened. In addition, we found a pair of tweezers and a needle, both of electrum (gold and silver alloy), and a great number of beads, of carnelian and tile. The whole collection seems to have been arranged in a wooden casket, now perished, which was probably covered with gold foil, some fragments of which we recovered on the spot. Three small rectangular gold plates, each with ten holes, probably for fixing nails, were found. These puzzled some of us at first, and the problem was not solved until the 1954–55 season when a further discovery of jewelry revealed the purpose of the little gold plates. The measurements were as follows (1) 1½″ by ¾″, (2) 1½″ by ¾″, (3) 1½″ by ¾″. Small fragments of gold leaf were also discovered. A large diorite bowl of porphyritic rock, with handles, lay near the deposit. These deposits had probably never been disturbed since they had been laid. They might well have belonged to a lady of the king's household.

Perhaps most people, when they think of golden objects found in an Egyptian tomb, recall the incredibly rich deposits found in the tomb of Tutankhamen, which included a coffin of solid gold weighing 300 pounds, besides numerous pieces of jewelry and ornaments of the same metal. But Tutankhamen lived some fifteen hundred years after the time when this pyramid was built. The period of Tutankhamen was a time of great conquests in Asia and the Sudan, conquests which brought in rich booty, and a time when the mines and quarries of the eastern desert and Nubia were fully exploited and gold was plentiful.

We do not expect to find such richness in a tomb of the Third Dynasty. Nevertheless, the mining and working of gold was known even in pre-dynastic times, and we know from the objects found in the tomb of Queen Hetephras, the wife of Snofru, which I shall discuss later, that in her time, the end of the Third and the beginning of the Fourth Dynasty, the art of the goldsmith had reached a very high level. But jewelry of this period is extremely rare, which is why the discovery of these Third Dynasty examples gave us so much pleasure. It also provided us with a valuable clue to the fact that, in spite of its unfinished state, *the pyramid had been used for burial.*

The Egyptians mined their gold at several places, but mainly in the eastern desert south of the Qena-Quseir road to the Sudan frontier. They found it in veins running through the quartz rock. "The ancient workings," writes Engelbach, "are enormous, their galleries having been pounded by balls of dolerite for hundreds of yards into the living rock." [1]

Some visitors to the pyramid, among them Leonard Cottrell, suggested that the presence in the entrance corridor of these valuable objects and the stone vessels, may indicate that the tomb had been robbed, or at least that an attempt at robbery had been made. Why, they asked, should such things be found in the corridor instead of

---

[1] R. Engelbach, "Mechanical and Technical Processes," Chapter 5 of *The Legacy of Egypt*, Oxford, Clarendon Press, 1942.

in tombs or store chambers leading off it, unless thieves
had attempted to remove them and had been interrupted?

My answer to such critics is this. The objects were
found under a thick layer of clay. The stone bowls, dishes,
etc., had been carefully arranged in layers with the clay
above them as a protection, and above this clay the builders
had piled the huge stones of the blockage which had been
thrown down the shaft to fill it. That blockage, I am convinced, had never been disturbed since the shaft was made
by the pyramid builders. Therefore the objects, including
the gold jewelry, must have been left there deliberately,
and not discarded by robbers. In any case, why should tomb
robbers have left behind such valuable and easily portable
objects as the golden bracelets and other trinkets, which
had lain in a wooden casket, traces of which still remain?

As for the reason for laying the trinket box in such a
position, there may, for all we know, be a tomb nearby.
At the time of writing the corridor has not been properly
cleared, and there may yet be other carefully concealed
shafts which have so far escaped detection.

These golden ornaments are the only jewelry which
has been preserved from the Third Dynasty, and so little
gold jewelry has survived from the Old Kingdom that this
collection is virtually unique. The only other Old Kingdom jewelry pieces known are the anklets and other be-
longings of Queen Hetephras, the mother of King Khufu,
found by Dr. G. A. Reisner in a deep shaft near the Great
Pyramid thirty years ago. But those are of later date.

I should explain at this point that, although I am

writing this narrative as far as possible in the order in which events happened, work is going on simultaneously at several points at once, and this will explain what might appear as inconsistencies in dating. For example, we had already begun in May to explore the corridor beyond the vertical shaft, but it was not until June that we found the jewelry, although we had already passed this point of the corridor some time earlier.

The next discovery was even more important archaeologically than the finding of the jewelry, although the objects themselves would have had little interest to the layman. They were simply small, conical, buff-colored pottery jars sealed with dried clay. The seals, used as stoppers for jars, are of great importance to archaeologists, for sometimes they are impressed with the name of the owner of the tomb.

Whenever I found such seals I carried them out and searched them carefully under a magnifying glass and in a strong light, for the seal, where it occurs, is usually faint and difficult to discern. During the early part of June I found five clay sealings bearing impressions from cylinder seals which gave the name of a hitherto unknown king. The hieroglyphic sign reads Sekhem-Khet ("Powerful of Body").

These sealings had to be handled with great delicacy for fear they might crumble and the vital evidence be destroyed, but when I had carefully cleaned them with a soft brush and treated them with fixative I was able to read the inscriptions and compare them.

As I said, the most plausible reading of the sign is Sekhem-Khet, but it is surprising to find the phonetic 's' written before the *sekhem* sign. At that period, and especially in a royal name, one would expect the *sekhem* sign alone.

Readers may be curious to know how it was possible to recognize that this was a *king's* name and not that of a lesser man. They may have read that in Ancient Egyptian inscriptions the royal name is enclosed within a framework in the shape of an elongated oval, called the cartouche (escutcheon), and is depicted in detailed inscriptions as a loop formed by a double thickness of rope, the end being tied together to form a straight line.

During the first four Dynasties the king bore three names. The first was the *Horus* name. This was inscribed within a rectangular frame with recessed paneling below; it was surmounted by a falcon. This was called the *serekh*; the frame represented the king's palace, and the falcon personified him as the earthly embodiment of the god Horus. Secondly there was the *nebti* name which displayed the king as identified with the two goddesses representing the two kingdoms of Upper and Lower Egypt. The third was the *n-sw-bit* name which means "King of Upper and Lower Egypt." From the Fourth Dynasty onward these two names were inserted within a cartouche. But the *serekh* —the frame surmounted by the falcon—remained in its original form down to the end of Ancient Egyptian history.

As Djoser's Horus name was Nether-er-Khet, there may be some connection, since the new king uses the same syllable as that of Djoser. It may be that he was of the same family as the latter king, though the presence of this syllable—Khet—does not necessarily prove it.

This king is completely unknown. His name does not appear on the Sakkara List preserved in the Cairo Museum, nor on the list of kings in the temple of Sethi Ist at Abydos, nor in the Turin Papyrus. Neither is he mentioned by Manetho. Non-Egyptologist readers may smile, but the discovery of this name of a hitherto unknown king of this remote dynasty meant almost as much to me as finding the pyramid itself! I took the precious pieces of clay back to the Rest House at Sakkara and studied them repeatedly. But there seemed no doubt of the fact that this was a "new" king.

As an example of how a fragment of dried clay can throw a ray of light on early Egyptian history, I should mention that in the Wady Maghara, in Sinai, there is an inscription on the rock containing a name which has been read as *Semer*-Khet, a known king of the First Dynasty. But the inscription is not at all clear, and it may be that the name is not *Semer*-Khet but that of this Third Dynasty king *Sekhem*-Khet; the fact that the inscription appears near a similar one bearing Djoser's name may be significant. However, I shall discuss this in more detail in my summarizing chapter at the end of this book.

The tiny scrap of evidence which I have found may not in itself seem important to the lay reader. But let him try to look at it in this way. Egyptology is like an enormous jigsaw puzzle in which there are many players. The discovery of the name of this unknown king is interesting and important, though it may not immediately have more significance than a fragment of the puzzle which can be fitted to another fragment. But perhaps at some future date another archaeologist of this or another generation may find that it is a vital clue to the solution of a major part of the puzzle. It is this, and not treasure hunting, which gives the Egyptologist his major satisfaction: the thought that he is contributing, in however small a way, to our knowledge of human history.

At a distance of 101' 9" from the entrance of the substructure, in the western wall of the main corridor and at a height of 3.28 feet above the floor of the corridor, we found a small doorway, measuring 4' 8" wide, which opened into a low side-passage, 17' 5" long. This led us to a T-shaped gallery containing 120 magazines or storage chambers. The vertical arm of the T (see plan), we found to be 134' long and about 5' wide. The horizontal arm, which runs north-south, is about 665' long and 5' wide. The compartments are cut in both sides of the horizontal arm of this gallery, in a "staggered" fashion, branching out from alternate sides, so as to permit the living rock to give support to the roof of the complex. The compartments on each side of the gallery are at regular intervals, and are approximately of the same dimensions.

There is an interesting resemblance here to the famous Layer Pyramid at Zawiyet-el-Eryan, briefly described in Chapter Two, but whereas in the latter structure the compartments were cut on one side only of the gallery, here they are cut alternately on *both* sides. Some stone and pottery vases were found at the entrance to the side passage leading from the entrance corridor. The whole complex is filled up to about two thirds of its height with debris, which has still to be cleared. We may find other objects under the debris, which consists of rock chippings from the ancient excavations.

Past the shaft the main corridor continued to descend into the depths beneath the pyramid, but its course was partly filled up with fragments of rock which had fallen from the ceiling and the sides. A glance at illustration 19 will convey far better than my words the condition of this corridor. When it was first cut, nearly five thousand years ago, it was no doubt roughly rectangular in section, with a sloping floor and a curved ceiling sloping down at the same angle. But in the course of centuries much of the rock had fallen from the roof and sides, so that as we see it today it looks more like a natural limestone cave such as one finds in the Pyrenees or the calcareous hills of central France.

Much of the rock is of very bad quality. The strata are soft and full of longitudinal fissures, filled with crystalized fibrous gypsum which gleamed in the light of our lamps. It was a slow job tunneling down, and I was grateful for my skilled men from Koptos, who, as we worked our way downward, supported the sides and roof of the corridor with masonry and timber props, so that it began to look like a mine gallery.

We were nearing the end of May, 1954. Normally

the "season" for excavation ends in April, because after that time the heat is too intense to make archaeological work practicable or comfortable, also because it is necessary to devote six or more months to the study and recording of discoveries. But in this case the interest was so great—as was also our determination to penetrate to the end of the entrance corridor and find what lay beyond —that we carried on some weeks beyond the time when the "season" would normally have ended.

During May we penetrated to a distance of 236' 3" from the entrance of the corridor. It was very hot in the depths beneath the pyramid, and we were working under difficult conditions. The corridor went down and down, and seemed to have no end. Then suddenly we were brought to a halt. Ahead of us lay a seemingly impervious mass of rock which at first baffled and depressed us, because it seemed that the corridor led nowhere and that there was no burial chamber. The rough, unfinished condition of the upper sides of the corridor pointed clearly to the fact that the pyramid substructure had never been completed, and it seemed only too likely that, having burrowed down to this great depth, the ancient builders had, for some reason, abandoned their work.

I was about to postpone further work in the passage until the next season, but my chief workman, Hofni Ibrahim, that veteran of many excavations, was in favor of carrying on.

"We are *fi galb el-haram*—in the heart of the pyramid," said he. "We should not stop." So we carried on.

A good deal of consolidation work was necessary before we could venture to remove the mass of rock at the far end, and some weeks were spent in the laborious task. Then, with the utmost care, we set to work on the rocky mass. When this had been cleared the outlines of a rock-cut doorway appeared and then a massive blockage of dry masonry, the third we had encountered, completely filling the doorway. We could not conceal our joy. There *was* something beyond the rocky mass, after all. Could one doubt that we were on the threshold of the sarcophagus chamber itself? But for me this joy was mingled with apprehension and anxiety, fear of the unknown and anxiety for what was forthcoming. So many Egyptian tombs had been found robbed. And in spite of the three intact blocking walls, I still feared that perhaps the ancient tomb robbers might have entered by another route.

On May 31, 1954, we made a hole in the upper half of the blockage. We found it was 10 feet thick, and much time was spent in laboriously removing the stones and passing them back. At last the final stone was removed and I crawled forward on my belly, electric torch in hand.

We had broken through the blockage near the roof of a large vault. Below was black emptiness. Without further hesitation I plunged, half falling, half scrambling, to the floor of the chamber.

NINE

The Sarcophagus Chamber

HOFNI FOLLOWED ME. WHEN WE HAD PICKED OURSELVES up and the lamp was raised, a wonderful sight greeted us. In the middle of a rough-cut chamber lay a magnificent sarcophagus of pale, golden, translucent alabaster. We moved toward it. My first thought was: "Is it intact?" Hurriedly, with my electric torch, I examined the top for the lid. But there was no lid; the top was of one piece with the rest.

This was unique in my experience as an Egyptologist. Normally sarcophagi are closed by a lid which fits over the top. But this sarcophagus was different. It had been carved out of a single block of alabaster, and the entrance was not at the top but at one of the ends facing the entrance to the chamber on its northern side. I knelt down and carefully examined this end.

It was sealed by an alabaster panel, roughly T-shaped —with a very broad vertical arm to the T and short projecting arms (see illustration 20), which had been slid into position from the top, presumably along vertical grooves cut in the side of the alabaster box. And to my amazement and delight it appeared to be quite intact. There were traces of plaster at the joins, and, unlike many sarcophagi, there were no traces of any attempt having been made to open it. Few sarcophagi of the Third Dynasty have survived. Firth and Quibell found two in Djoser's pyramid, and these were of similar design to this one, except that they had lids. This, I was tolerably certain, was a Third Dynasty sarcophagus, contemporary with the pyramid and not a later intrusion.

The smooth top was obscured with rock dust and small fragments which had fallen from the roof. Much larger pieces lay about the floor of the chamber, any one of which might have smashed or seriously damaged the alabaster box, but by a miracle the sarcophagus had escaped. Near the northern end, on the top, lay the decayed and carbonized fragments of some plant or shrub, arranged roughly in the form of a V (see illustration 21). This would appear to be the remains of a funerary wreath, left there, presumably, by those who placed the sarcophagus in the chamber 4,700 years ago.

It was all too wonderful to be true, and for some time Hofni and I stood staring in amazement at the lonely alabaster box, the loveliness of which was all the more striking in contrast with the rough, unfinished walls of the chamber.

Then, one by one, my other workmen clambered through the hole in the blockage and scrambled down into the chamber. They were mad with excitement and, catching their enthusiasm, I gave way completely to my pent-up feelings, kept in check for so long. We danced around the sarcophagus and wept. We embraced each other. It was a very strange moment in that dark chamber, 130 feet beneath the surface of the desert. As I have said, many of these workmen had been employed by great archaeologists such as Reisner and Junker and Petrie, and they told me that never in their whole lives had they seen such a thing. They were mad with joy, for this was the crowning of three years of patient work, in an area which at first had not looked at all promising. We had had many ups and downs, but now success seemed to be in sight.

And then, suddenly, when the first excitement was over, we became very quiet, and we stood at a distance from the sarcophagus with great respect and awe toward the king who we all believed was buried there. We recited parts of the Koran, and asked God for benevolence toward the king. All the men showed the greatest reverence.

After this I made a careful examination of the chamber. It is roughly rectangular with a north-south axis of 79′ 2″ and an east-west axis of 17′ 2″. The height is about 17′. The floor was covered with a thick layer of soft clay. Originally, perhaps, the whole corridor and the chamber were so covered, the clay being moistened so that the sarcophagus could easily be slid down the sloping corridor. It may have been that wooden sledges were impracticable in the pyramid, but in any case, even if they had been used, the lubricant would have helped. As the chamber was never finished, the builders did not remove the clay —an example of how the archaeologist can learn from an unfinished building facts which could not be learned from a completed structure.

Examination of illustration 20 will show the rough-cut niches on the eastern and western sides of the chamber. They extended from floor to ceiling. They open on each side of the chamber, opposite the center of the long sides of the sarcophagus; their purpose is unknown.

The chamber was clearly never finished. The walls are roughly hewn out of the rock as a preliminary to shaping and smoothing. The roof is horizontal, and bears the mark of the masons' chisels. There is a red line traced along the north-south axis of the ceiling. Part of the eastern and western walls have been faced with coarse masonry to repair defects. Probably it was the intention of the builders to smooth the walls and to cover them with glazed tiles as in some of the corridors of Djoser's pyramid.

The chamber is surrounded by a complex of unfinished galleries, the plan of which is like a three-pronged fork, the middle prong extending farther southward than those on each side. The middle prong of the fork extends southward from the southern side of the chamber for a distance of 60' 8". This gallery is almost in line with the entrance corridor, but not quite; it is 25' 7". The width of the gallery is 4' 11".

The base of the fork consists of two galleries projecting from the sarcophagus chamber immediately south of the entrance corridor. They run in an east-west direction for an over-all distance of about 75' 6". At the end of each of the short arms there is a right-angled corner, and the galleries turn to the south, running parallel with the central gallery and forming the outer prongs of the fork. They are almost but not quite of equal length. The western gallery is 64′ 2″ long, whereas the eastern gallery measures 66′ 6″. The western gallery is 6′ 2″ wide, but the eastern gallery is broader—8′ 3″.

Now look at the plan again. It will be seen that there is another gallery, 27′ 1″ long and 6′ wide leading from the northern wall of the west arm of the east-west gallery and which admits to yet another gallery 38′ 9″ long and 9′ 10″ wide. From this a narrower passage leads eastward as if to join the entrance corridor, but it stops short of it by 8.27″. A thin wall of rock divides it from the corridor. It would seem that the original intention of the builders was to join the two galleries, but that work was stopped.

The floors of these galleries were covered with the debris from the cutting of the rock, which had not been removed by the builders as it would have been had the substructure been finished. Every indication pointed to a sudden cessation of the work, for a reason which we do not yet know—probably the premature death of the king for whom the monument was being prepared.

We spent several days exploring these dark galleries, but after a most exhaustive search I failed to find any evidence of another entrance made by tomb robbers. The only entrance to the pyramid was through the main corridor, which we had found blocked in three places. A further indication that the chamber was intact was the presence, in front of the third blocking wall, of a fall of rock which had not been disturbed. At last I was able to satisfy myself beyond any shadow of doubt that we were the first to enter the sarcophagus chamber since its makers left it.

The galleries, like those under Djoser's pyramid, seem to have been intended as habitations for the king's ka, and perhaps to contain funerary furniture and equipment. Nothing has so far been found, but there is much work ahead clearing the debris, under which we may find objects. Also I must emphasize that these are not necessarily the only galleries which will be found. One has only to think of the warren of tunnels and passages beneath Djoser's structure, which are so numerous and complicated that even today many of them have been incompletely explored. It is unwise for an archaeologist to speculate, but when we have cleared down to the floor of the entrance corridor, the sarcophagus chamber, and the surrounding galleries, it is not impossible that we may find shafts leading to other passages at a different level. There are precedents for this in Djoser's Step Pyramid.

From the same example we may expect to find other galleries, unconnected with those surrounding the sarcophagus chamber and approached by separate entrances, perhaps leading to other chambers intended for the burial of the king's family. Others may exist beneath the great enclosure outside the pyramid. But all this is mere conjecture, and many more seasons of excavation will be necessary before we can say that the pyramid has yielded all its secrets.

The Director-General of the Antiquities Service came to see the sarcophagus, but after that no one was admitted to the pyramid except fellow archaeologists from the Department of Antiquities, my workmen and myself. From the time we first opened the pyramid substructure special precautions had been taken to guard the monument against any possibility of theft. Sudanese soldiers of the Egyptian Frontier Force were placed on guard, reliable and trustworthy men who had previously guarded the excavations of Professor Montet at Tanis, when he found the magnificent silver coffin of King Psusennes and other treasures. A guard post was built on the ridge overlooking the pyramid entrance, and soldiers patrolled the area day and night. A strong iron door was fixed at the pyramid entrance, and at the end of every day, before leaving the pyramid, each man who had worked within it was searched. On these occasions, I always made a point of being the first to be searched.

Having examined and measured the galleries and chamber, I then began to study the sarcophagus in greater detail. I compared it with those found by Firth and Quibell in Djoser's pyramid, and found that there were close similarities, although they had had lids whereas this had the sliding panel. They were found at the far end of one of the galleries running in a westerly direction under Djoser's mastaba (*see* Chapter One). They are described by the discoverers as follows:

The first coffin is without inscription or decoration, barrel-roofed with square ends. In each of these ends two holes are pierced and joined below by semi-circular channels; through these ran the ropes by which the lid was manipulated into place; then the ropes were withdrawn and the holes stopped with alabaster plugs. These plugs were found . . . the north-east and south-east lower corners had been damaged and repaired with ingeniously cut patches.

The second sarcophagus is more interesting; it lay inside the end chamber, at right angles to the first . . . on a limestone base flanged on the sides but not on the ends, just such a stone as we had found tipped up at the east end of another chamber.[1]

Within this second sarcophagus Firth and Quibell found the fragmented remains of a wooden coffin which had been plated with gold, but the tomb had been robbed in antiquity, as usual, and little remained but minute pieces of decayed six-ply wood, and small pieces of the gold facing mixed with rubble. This was the first example of plywood ever found. In the middle of the debris the excavators found the skeleton of a child of some eight or nine years of age. An interesting point which bears directly on what we discovered later regarding the interior of the new sarcophagus is that this example found by Firth and Quibell "was stained over considerable areas with parallel vertical lines in black caused by long contact with the . . . outermost layer of the coffin."

---

[1] C. M. Firth and J. E. Quibell, *The Step Pyramid*, Vol. I, pp. 41–2.

Our sarcophagus is flat-topped, not barrel-roofed, and the external dimensions are:

length: 7′ 9″
breadth: 3′ 9″
height: 3′ 6″

considerably longer than the first sarcophagus found by Firth and Quibell. They do not give the dimensions of the second, but it is also small, having been made for a child. The "holes . . . joined below by semi-circular channels" have a parallel in the newly discovered sarcophagus, but in this case they are in the top of the sliding panel, and were also clearly intended for ropes by which the panel was raised and lowered (it weighs 500 pounds). Like those found in Djoser's pyramid, our sarcophagus is uninscribed, and in form and workmanship bears close similarity to them.[2]

The repairs which Firth and Quibell noted at the corners of one of the sarcophagi which they discovered are almost paralleled in the new one. The upper northwest corner had been broken in antiquity and repaired by inserting two new pieces of alabaster of the same quality. The upper northeast corner and the lower northeast corners were also broken, but the original pieces had been replaced and cemented into position with plaster. A defect in the top of the sarcophagus at the west side near its

---

[2] There are also two sarcophagi found at Dashur by de Morgan which in every detail and dimension are all but identical with those found in Djoser's pyramid, and which also resemble the one which I have found. These, attributed by de Morgan to the Middle Kingdom, are now believed to date from the Third or Fourth Dynasty.

south end was filled up with gypsum plaster, which had been smoothed and colored to match the alabaster. Alabaster is a soft material, and the sarcophagus might have been damaged when it was being dragged down the corridor, and subsequently repaired *in situ*. Incidentally this is the first known use of gypsum plaster in Ancient Egyptian history.

The sarcophagus was made from a single block of alabaster, which bears on the top of the southern end marks made by a saw in a chevron shape. All sides were polished, but the makers had not managed to remove this blemish on the upper side. With its soft, translucent texture, delicate veinings which are sometimes golden, sometimes rose-color according to the lighting, this is one of the earliest and most beautiful examples ever found of a royal Egyptian sarcophagus.

That it was intended for a royal burial I have no doubt. The smaller sarcophagi found in the step pyramid were in one of the many subsidiary galleries, probably intended for members of the royal family. This one was found exactly in the center of a large chamber which, as we subsequently found by measurement, lies exactly under the place where the peak of the pyramid would have stood had it been completed.

Alabaster, or calcite, was quarried in several places in Egypt. The best-known quarry was at a place called in the ancient inscriptions Het-nub. It is in the eastern desert some fourteen miles southeast of El-Amarna, in Middle Egypt. There one can still see the gigantic pit cut down into the rock to a depth of more than 60 feet and approached by a narrow road. The names of the overseers. and the kings who sent them, can still be seen near the entrance passage. Some date back to the Fourth Dynasty. Alabaster being a soft rock, it was relatively easy to quarry, but the selection of the best quality of stone, and its working and polishing, must have required great technical skill and artistry.

After noticing the resemblances between the masonry of Djoser's pyramid and enclosure and those of the new monument, *e.g.*, a similar type of enclosure wall with bastions and panels, accretion walls with the courses inclined inward, etc., we noted the differences, also. Djoser's burial chamber, though it lay beneath the pyramid, was constructed of granite blocks at the bottom of an open pit, which was afterward filled up with masonry. But this chamber was hewed out of the living rock, and approached by a long, sloping corridor. Again, Djoser's body, if it was buried in its chamber (and there seems little doubt of this), was almost certainly not enclosed in a sarcophagus. But here was a sealed sarcophagus in the central chamber of the new pyramid, the obvious place for a king's burial.

A third point: the entrance gallery leading to Djoser's burial chamber was completely blocked with masonry and rubble. Here the passage had been sealed only at three points: at the entrance, near the vertical shaft, and at the entrace to the sarcophagus chamber itself. In some ways, as I have said, the new pyramid resembled most closely the southern or layer pyramid at Zawiyeat-el-Eryan, particularly in the arrangement of the T-shaped galleries to the north, though in that case the storage chambers led from one side of the gallery only, whereas in this structure they branched off alternately from both sides. There, says Reisner, "the form of the entrance and the plan of the underground chambers are like those in private stairway tombs of Dynasty III. The entrance descends in a sloping passage from the west, then turns at right angles to the south and descends 147' 8" to a room cut in the rock underneath the masonry."

The abandonment of the pit construction in favor of a rock-hewn chamber may, like the use of larger stones in constructing the new pyramid, indicate a later date than that of Djoser, but it will be some time before we can establish the exact chronological position of King Sekhem-Khet in the sequence of Third Dynasty kings.

TEN

Preparations for the Opening

WE ENTERED THE SARCOPHAGUS CHAMBER ON MAY 31, 1954, but did not open the sarcophagus until June 27. It may be asked why we allowed nearly a month to elapse before seeking an answer to the question which was in all our minds: "Does the sarcophagus contain the body of a king?" The answer is that archaeology is not a treasure hunt but a search for knowledge, and there were many things to be done, photographs to be taken, measurements made, chemical analyses carried out, before we took the next step. And quite apart from these considerations, we were still not quite satisfied with the state of the entrance corridor; more consolidation work had to be done before it was considered safe for the press and the public to enter the pyramid.

During those four anxious weeks, while my workmen built masonry and timber supports for those parts of the walls and roof which needed it, I spent many hours inside the pyramid, scrutinizing every inch of the substructure, taking notes, supervising photography, preparing measured diagrams, and, in the evenings when the day's work

127

was over, studying the finds, discussing them with other archaeologists, forming and rejecting theories.

All this was done under a spotlight of publicity. I suppose that, fifty years ago or more, archaeologists such as Borchardt and Quibell had little to distract them from their main task. But ever since the discovery of the tomb of Tutankhamen in 1922 there has arisen a world-wide curiosity about Ancient Egypt. From the discovery of the entrance corridor, the press of the world had shown a flattering interest in our work. Journalists from many countries arrived almost daily at my Rest House, eager to obtain the latest news for their readers. The American magazine *Life* generously contributed six thousand dollars for the furtherance of the work, and its representatives, a writer and a photographer, were often at my side. Then there were representatives of *The Times* of London, who have always shown an informed interest in Egyptian excavations, and other journalists representing such world-famous journals as *Il Tempo* of Italy, *Paris-Match* of France, *The New York Times*, and leading periodicals and newspapers of Germany, Scandinavia, and even from as far off as the Argentine and Brazil.

On most days I had hardly time to dress and have breakfast before the crunch of car tires on the gravel outside my house would announce the arrival of a new party of visitors. Nor was this all. Telephone calls and telegrams flowed in from many parts of the world, and the bewildered operator at the village post office at Badrashein, who rarely receives a call from anywhere farther than Cairo, picked up his receiver one morning to hear a voice speaking to him from a place called New York, U.S.A.!

I have heard some archaeologists deplore all this. But, although I admit that it can be embarrassing at times and sometimes adds a heavy burden to the duties of the archaeologist, I think this interest should be welcomed and encouraged. The days when Egyptology was the pastime of a few wealthy men who employed professional Egyptologists have long passed, and the deeper and more widespread becomes the interest and knowledge of our work among the general public, the better it will be for our science. I must add at this point that I deeply appreciate the encouragement which has been given to me and to other Egyptian archaeologists by our Government. This has made my work possible.

Having admitted this, I must confess that there were times when I have sympathized with Mr. Howard Carter, the discoverer of the tomb of Tutankhamen, who described vividly in his book [1] the difficulties he encountered from the overzealous attentions of the press in his time. "The scene at the tomb," wrote a contemporary correspondent, "awakened memories of Derby Day. The road leading to the rock-enclosed ravine . . . was packed with vehicles and animals of every variety. The guides, donkey-boys, sellers of antiquities, and hawkers of lemonade were doing a roaring trade. . . . When the last articles had been removed from the corridor today the newspaper corre-

---

[1] *The Tomb of Tut-ankh-amen,* Cassell, London.

spondents began a spirited dash across the desert to the banks of the Nile upon donkeys, horses, camels, and chariot-like sand-carts in a race to be the first to reach the telegraph office. . . ."

Carter himself wrote:

> There were many days last season in which we actually had ten parties of visitors, and if we had given way to every demand there would not have been a day in which we did not exceed the ten. In other words there would have been weeks at a time when no work would have been done at all.

When I was Chief Inspector of Antiquities at Luxor and leading a fairly quiet life, I sometimes read those lines with a certain envy, but after my experiences in 1953 and 1954, when the press of the world arrived daily at the door of my lonely house at Sakkara, I began to see Carter's point. To be asked to do serious scientific work, needing much care and thought, with visitors constantly arriving, was like being asked to conduct a delicate surgical operation with a crowd of eager spectators jogging one's elbow. May I therefore take this opportunity gently to point out to my friends of the press and other interested visitors that archaeology is a slow and difficult task, and that it is not always possible, and never wise, to give "snap answers" to questions to which replies can only be given after long and patient thought? Also that the excavator *must*, if he is to do his work properly, be given ample time for study and reflection?

Preparations for the Opening

There was one branch of "public relations" with which Carter did not have to deal in his day but which now presents another problem to archaeologists, and that is radio and television. Representatives of several of the leading radio broadcasting companies of the Middle East, of Europe, and of America arrived with their tape recorders, and day-to-day accounts of the progress of the excavations were broadcast in many languages. Most of these radio men were concerned principally with news broadcasts during the progress of the work, though the Egyptian State Radio produced an informative program on the excavations as a whole. It is also to the credit of the British Broadcasting Corporation that, in addition to their resident correspondent, Bernard Forbes, they sent out one of their most distinguished documentary writers, Leonard Cottrell, who spent a month with me and prepared a complete recorded program on the work. This eventually was broadcast both on the British domestic wave lengths and in many countries of the British Commonwealth. Such is the interest shown in Egyptology today by the general public throughout the world.

There were also television and film camera units.

I firmly believed that the sarcophagus contained a body, and I was supported in this belief by several eminent Egyptologists.

Let us examine the evidence up to this date. Here we had an unfinished pyramid which, from the evidence provided by later burials, had remained untouched and probably unknown for at least three thousand years. The entrance was sealed with a massive wall of dry masonry, which also had not been touched since the day it was built. Within the pyramid the entrance corridor was sealed at two other points, and these sealings also were intact. At the heart of the pyramid was an unfinished chamber, from which there was no exit save the sealed corridor. It contained a sarcophagus which, from its form and design, was clearly made in the Third Dynasty, contemporary with the pyramid itself. And that sarcophagus was closed by a sliding panel which was firmly cemented into position. The only logical conclusion was that the sarcophagus contained a body, and that the body was most likely that of the king for whom the monument was built, a king whose name we had already discovered.

The chief point which worried me at first was the presence, at the top of the vertical construction shaft, of animal remains accompanied by papyri of Saitic date, two thousand years after the presumed date when the pyramid was built. But the pit containing the animal bones was merely scooped out of the top of the filling; the rest was untouched. Therefore, it seemed to me, even if the Saites had known of the existence of the pyramid, they had not penetrated to the interior.

Another objection which was raised at the time by a few persons was that the sarcophagus might contain what we call an "intrusive burial," *i.e.*, a burial introduced into the pyramid at a later date than that of its construction. We know that the Ancient Egyptians were not above usurping their predecessors' monuments when the occasion served, and there are numerous examples of such intrusive burials. But all the available data contradicted this theory. There was the sarcophagus, which, as I have pointed out by reference to the sarcophagi found in Djoser's pyramid, was of a type associated with the Third Dynasty. There was also another equally cogent reason for rejecting this suggestion. When the Ancient Egyptians usurped an ancient tomb they would first light a fire in the burial chamber to drive out the spirit of the previous owner. In my experience as an archaeologist I have frequently found evidences of this custom, as have other excavators.

This sarcophagus chamber in the newly discovered pyramid had clearly never been entered since the day its makers left it. The walls were rough and unfinished, still bearing the paint marks and leveling lines left by the ancient quarrymen. The walls bore no traces of soot which would have remained had the chamber been usurped by a later intruder. After the most careful consideration, and after examining and rejecting every alternative theory—robbery, usurpation, etc.—I was left with the conclusion that the sarcophagus was intact, and would almost certainly contain a body.

There was also the significant evidence of the funeral wreath, suggesting that, after the last rites had been performed, those who buried the king had left this farewell tribute, just as the mourners who followed the coffin of Tutankhamen, thirteen centuries later, left behind in the tomb wreaths of flowers and shrubs.

During this critical period, when I was frequently asked by the press to give definite replies to questions which could not always be decisively answered, I was heartened and encouraged by the interest shown in the excavations by distinguished archaeologists from Europe and the New World. Dr. Hans Stock of the University of Munich and Dr. Elmar Edel of the University of Heidelberg came out to Egypt specially to see the discovery. They agreed with me in the reading of the king's name, and that all the evidence pointed to the fact that the monarch had been buried within the enclosure. They also confirmed that the sarcophagus chamber had never been entered since the last rituals were performed for the king. I was also honored by the visit of Dr. William C. Hayes, Curator of the Egyptian Department of the Metropolitan Museum of Art, New York, who supported the views of his fellow scholars from Europe.

Accurate observation and faithful recording are preliminary to any reconstruction. The prime duty of the field archaeologist is to collect and set in order material with not all of which he can himself deal at first hand. In no case will the last word be with him; and just because this is so his publication of the material must be minutely detailed, so that from it others may draw not only corroboration of his views but fresh conclusions and more light.[2]

I have always tried to follow this wise principle laid down by that great scholar and archaeologist, Sir Leonard

[2] Sir Leonard Woolley, *Digging up the Past*, p. 118, London, 1949.

Woolley, many years ago. Therefore, even though I was as anxious as any newspaperman or visitor to open the alabaster box, I had first to assure myself that every available fact had been recorded, every measurement and photograph taken, and every preparation made for the scientific observation and recording of the opening when the day arrived. All archaeology is in certain ways destruction, even at times destruction of evidence. This is less true in a solid building like a pyramid than in, say, a field excavation of mud-brick buildings. None the less, even in a half-finished structure such as this one, apparently devoid of large funerary objects, there was much to keep our experts busy.

At every stage of the work photographs were taken by Hasaballa el-Tayeb, official photographer of the Department of Antiquities at Sakkara. Careful measurements were taken of the corridor and its adjoining galleries. Geologists examined the rock strata through which the corridor passed, and took away samples of the crystals. The bones of sacrificed animals found in the vertical shaft were sent to zoologists for scrutiny. I carefully removed a small portion of the carbonized remains of the funerary wreath, and sent them to Mrs. V. Laurent Tackholm for provisional examination. Her preliminary report was that this might belong to the species *ferula*, a native of Libya. This was a fragrant shrub which was imported into Ancient Egypt for resin. The specific plant appears to be *asafetida*. A further specimen was sent to Professor Gaumann at Zurich for minute examination and classification.

Another specimen of the carbonized remains of this plant was sent to America for dating by the radio-carbon system. This is a method recently brought into use for estimating the age of material which once formed part of living matter. It has already yielded some interesting results in regard to Egyptian dating. Briefly, it operates in the following way.

The earth is continually being bombarded by cosmic rays, which convert the ordinary carbon (atomic weight 12) of carbon dioxide into another form of carbon (atomic weight 14) which is radioactive and gradually disintegrates. The amount of radio-carbon present in the atmosphere is roughly equal to that expected if it was mixed throughout all living matter, and if the cosmic rays had been of constant intensity for the last few thousand years.

When an organism dies, no further radio-carbon is added, and the amount present in the dead organism will gradually disintegrate according to known laws. After about 5,000 years (the half-life period) the amount will be reduced by one half. Thus, by determining the proportion of radio-carbon present in, for example, a specimen of wood, it is possible to estimate the period which has elapsed since the death of the tree of which it formed part. Plant material and wood, charcoal, burnt bone, dung and peat have been found useful. It is necessary to take great care to prevent contamination by substances likely to affect the results. The method is being applied in the dating of prehistoric sites such as the recently discovered cave at Lascaux in France, where carbon from an occupational level yielded an age date of 15,510 plus or minus 900 years.

Here are some results obtained from specimens of wood taken from Ancient Egyptian tombs.

Material	Source	Approximate Age in Years	Radio-carbon Age in Years
(1) Acacia wood	Tomb of Djoser	4,650	3,979 plus or minus 350 years
(2) Cypress wood	Tomb of Snofru	4,575	4,802 plus or minus 210 years
(3) Wood from roof beams	Tomb of the Vizier Hemaka	4,900	4,883 plus or minus 200 years

With the exception of the specimen from the Tomb of Djoser it will be seen that the results are in fair agreement with the generally accepted dates.

The specimen of the funeral wreath is being examined by the radio-carbon method to see if it agrees with my estimated date of the pyramid; if so it will indicate that the wreath was laid on the sarcophagus at the time it was first placed in the burial chamber, and not at a later date.

Specimens of the plaster used in repairing and sealing the sarcophagus and of the mortar used in the unfinished enclosure wall were sent to Dr. Zaky Iskander, of the Department of Antiquities, for chemical analysis. Here is a summary of his report:

(1) *Plaster from the front side.* Very white and was used for sticking the broken parts of the sarcophagus. Very

compact; has the appearance of artificial plaster. The sample proved to be powdered calcium phosphate, of the pure variety, containing traces of calcium sulphate and mixed with glue as an adhesive.

(2) *Plaster from the pinkish restoration of the sarcophagus.* This is an ordinary gypsum plaster which contains a little calcium carbonate and calcium phosphate, and some silica, and ferric and aluminum oxide.

(3) *Plaster from the north unfinished enclosure wall.* Mostly composed of powdered limestone with an adhesive of which very small traces are present and could not definitely be identified.

On June seventeenth the press was admitted to the pyramid for the first time. Before nine in the morning, the cars carrying the journalists, cameramen and radio reporters could be seen glinting along the valley road, then turning to climb the steep stony track to the necropolis. By nine thirty more than a hundred persons were gathered around the deep rectangular pit which led to the entrance doorway: Egyptians, Americans, Englishmen, Frenchmen, Italians, Syrians, both men and women. Some carried cameras, others tape recorders, other trailed cable. The walls of the pit echoed with the clamor of their voices as they pressed against the iron grille at which the smiling Sudanese soldiers kept guard.

I went down into the pyramid with Hussein and Hofni, then signaled for the first batch to be admitted. The original arrangement was that only ten people should be allowed to enter at one time, but it soon became evident that, once inside the pyramid, the journalists were not in any hurry to depart, and if we had stuck to our original plan a whole day would hardly have been sufficient to allow everyone to see the sarcophagus chamber. As a few clambered out along the steeply sloping corridor a greater number poured in, so that before long the chamber was crowded. I have asked a friend to allow me to quote from a letter he wrote at the time, describing the scene.

There must have been at least sixty people in that chamber when I first saw it. . . . In the centre of the floor stood the sarcophagus, a plain rectangular block of alabaster with the most beautiful, delicate veinings varying from gold to rose-colour. Around this lovely, lonely object the journalists clustered, sweat pouring off their faces, for it was extremely hot in the chamber 130 feet below the surface of the desert. Some leaned on the sarcophagus, others tried to peer under it; some perched themselves in the galleries which led off on four sides and poised their cameras. There was a continual winking of powerful flash-bulbs, a whirring of cine-cameras and babel of voices talking in several languages, French, English, and Arabic. . . . Goneim stood near the end of the sarcophagus, dressed in his khaki tunic and sun-hat, trying to make his voice heard above the din.

It was all so very different from the day when Hofni and I first stumbled into the chamber, the day when we had stood reverently around the sarcophagus and recited from the Koran. I was flattered by the publicity which was being given to my discovery, after three years of work which had been hardly noticed except by my fellow scholars and the learned journals. But when the last visitor had driven off to write his report and I had locked the door of the pyramid behind me, it was with relief that I drove back to my house, had a bath, and went to sleep.

By the end of the third week of June all preparations for the opening of the sarcophagus were complete. I discussed with Dr. Mustapha Amer the possibility of performing the opening in the presence of the press, as had been suggested. Wisely, in my opinion, it was decided to open it first only in the presence of senior officials of the Department. It would have been extremely difficult to carry out this delicate task surrounded by cameras, microphones and eager reporters. We had no idea what might be the condition of the coffin and the mummy, should they be found, and elaborate precautions were taken to photograph the interior of the sarcophagus at the instant of opening, for fear lest the inrush of air might cause the remains to disintegrate.

The last few days were nerve-wracking. The newspapers began to come in with such headlines as "From a Pharaoh's Tomb Comes a Gleam of Gold" and "Golden Riddle of the Unfinished Pyramid." I began to long for the day when the mystery would be solved, one way or the other.

ELEVEN

The Mystery
of the Sarcophagus

IT WILL BE DIFFICULT TO WRITE THIS CHAPTER WITHOUT
appearing overdramatic; but I must attempt it. Imagine,
then, a small party of men gathered at the entrance to
the pyramid on the morning of June twenty-sixth. Among
them was Dr. Mustapha Amer, the Director of the Department of Antiquities, Mr. Zaky Saad, also of the
Department, Mr. Mohamon-ad Mahdi, and Dr. Zaky
Iskander, and my chief workmen, Hofni Ibrahim and Hussein Ibrahim, who had worked with me for three long
years. This was to be, perhaps, the climax of all our efforts.
As I walked down the long corridor which I had traversed
so many times, my feelings were mixed—relief that the
tension was soon to be ended; hope of a great discovery;
anxiety lest, after all, I was to be disappointed.

We spoke very little until we entered the chamber
where the sarcophagus lay, and once again I stopped to
admire the beauty of the simple alabaster box the sides
of which reflected the brilliant light of the electric lamps
which we had installed within the chamber. At the north-

ern end, nearest the entrance doorway, we had erected a
scaffolding from which hung a large pulley. Over this a
rope was passed at the end of which were two steel hooks
which I had had specially made for insertion into the two
holes at the top of the sliding panel. My workmen carefully arranged the lights, and the cameras were placed
in position. Other members of the Department stood by
with chemical preservatives for use if necessary.

I thought of other archaeologists who had stood on
the brink of great discoveries: Carter when he opened the
sealed antechamber of the tomb of Tutankhamen; Reisner
when he found the deeply hid burial cache of Queen
Hetephras. I exchanged glances with Hofni and Hussein,
and knew what they, too, were feeling.

At last all was ready, and I gave the order to begin
the operation. Two of my workmen began to haul on the
rope, while others applied crowbars to the crack between
the lower part of the panel and the sarcophagus. The men
heaved with all their might; there was a scraping of metal
on stone. Nothing happened, the panel was wedged tightly
in position. The men heaved again, but for a long time the
heavy panel resisted all our efforts to move it.

Then at last it began to move, a mere inch or so.
Wedges were inserted in the aperture, and I carefully
examined the panel to make sure that no damage had
been done. I was right in my assumption that there were
vertical ribs running down each side of the panel, sliding
in grooves. I gave the order to continue. In all six men

were at work on raising the panel, but such was its weight (about 500 pounds), and the tightness with which it was sealed with a mixture of gypsum plaster and glue, that nearly two hours had passed before at last it slowly began to go up. I went down on my knees and looked inside.

The sarcophagus was empty.

I rose to my feet bewildered, and stood for some time looking at the sarcophagus in silence. My companions, too, said nothing. The thing was at first beyond my comprehension. Robbery? How could the sarcophagus have been robbed when the three blocking walls were intact and the alabaster box was sealed? It did not make sense. Again I knelt down and looked inside with the aid of a powerful lamp. The interior was quite pure and stainless. It had not been polished, as had the outer side, and still bore the marks of the tubular drills used in its making. If it had ever contained a coffin, surely it would bear some marks, as in the sarcophagus discovered by Firth in the Pyramid of Djoser (see Chapter Six). The more I examined this empty sarcophagus the more convinced I became that it had never contained a body. Yet there was the funerary wreath on the top. How did one explain that?

But for the time being there was nothing more to be done. Photographs were taken, and Dr. Zaky Iskander of the Chemical Laboratory took samples of the dust lying in the bottom inner side of the sarcophagus in the right-hand corner. Then, slowly and thoughtfully, we climbed back up the corridor and out into the burning sunlight.

The Prime Minister of Egypt, Lieutenant-Colonel Gamal Abdel Nasser, was, of course, informed that the sarcophagus was empty and that no treasure had been found inside. He graciously replied: "We are not interested in treasure. We are coming to Sakkara to see the sarcophagus, to promote scientific research, and to encourage Egyptian archaeologists."

He came with his staff and spent some time with me in the sarcophagus chamber, while I explained my theories. This encouragement from our Prime Minister greatly heartened us all in our work and took away some of the disappointment. We were now even more determined to get to the bottom of the mystery.

The press were informed, and soon headlines announced the disappointing news to the world. One paper headed its report: "Pharaoh Fiasco," another "They Dig for Three Years and Find Nothing." The more serious journals, such as *The Times* of London, were more sympathetic, and sought to find an answer to the problem. But on the whole the more popular papers naturally lost interest in the pyramid from the moment it was clear that the sarcophagus did not contain "the golden treasure of Pharaoh."

As for me, I admit that it was a bitter blow at first. Admittedly I had had the satisfaction of discovering a new pyramid, and the name of a hitherto unknown king of the Third Dynasty. Archaeologically that was in itself a triumph. Also, I knew that the work had scarcely begun and that there must be other subterranean galleries to explore. None the less, I must confess to a keen disappointment at not finding the body of the king in the expected place.

In the expected place. . . . But had one a right ever to expect anything so definite when dealing with the monuments of the Ancient Egyptians? They were a cunning people, skilled in deception, and the history of excavation is full of examples of blind alleys, false doorways, traps and stratagems to deceive the tomb robbers. Perhaps they had never intended to bury the king in the pyramid? But then there was the blocked entrance corridor, and the fact that the chamber would have been precisely beneath the peak of the structure had this been completed. There was the example of Djoser's very similar structure, which the king was almost certainly interred in the burial chamber beneath the pyramid. And there was that golden jewelry, suggesting that the pyramid had definitely been used for burial. How could one account for that?

These and many other thoughts passed through my mind during the days and weeks that followed the opening. The season was now over, and there could be no more excavation until the coming autumn. But while I busied myself with the final preparations for the closing of the pyramid, my mind rarely left the problem of the empty sarcophagus. Somehow I was determined to get to the bottom of the mystery.

The idea of robbery was clearly absurd. If the tomb had been robbed, would the robbers have taken the trouble to close and reseal the sarcophagus and rebuild the three blocking walls? It was inconceivable. A plundered tomb is a scene of devastation, the sarcophagus split open, fragments of funerary furniture lying about, the chamber often pierced by holes made by the robbers to effect their illicit entry. No, that was not the solution.

But the pyramid was obviously unfinished. Could it be that the builders had brought the sarcophagus into the chamber, left it there, and then resealed the corridor to await the death of the king, when it would be reopened to admit the mummy? And then, for some reason or other, the king was buried in another tomb?

But if that were so, why had they slid the panel into place and sealed it with plaster, making it extremely difficult to open? Why not have left the panel off until it was needed? And if not for burial, for what purpose had the chamber been designed?

Then there were the plant remains which looked very much like a funerary wreath. Would the Ancient Egyptians have placed a wreath on the sarcophagus unless the appropriate burial rites had been performed? Yet the sarcophagus had clearly never contained a body. Here was another mystery.

Then I thought of the first blocking wall, which, as will be remembered, was built in two parts (see Chapter Seven). I had thought at the time that the reason for this was that after taking the sarcophagus into the chamber the builders had partly closed the entrance, leaving enough space to admit the mummy when the actual burial took place. It seemed at the time the most likely explanation. But why had they bothered to do this if it had never been intended to bury the king under the pyramid? But perhaps it *had* been intended to do this, and there had been a change of plan? Was that a partial solution? We know from other Ancient Egyptian monuments that the builders often changed their plans during construction. Could it be that the original intention was to bury King Sekhem-Khet under his pyramid, but that for some reason the plan was changed and that he was finally buried elsewhere, perhaps under the outer enclosure? Then I remembered the White Wall, which had originally terminated the northern end of the pyramid enclosure, but had subsequently been covered up. An extension had been built on the northern side—again clear evidence of a change of plan by the original builders (see Chapter Four). Might not this be linked in some way with the apparent change in the arrangements for the burial?

It was annoying to have to halt the excavation at a point when there were so many questions which required answers—problems which further investigations might help to solve. But further work was, for the moment, out of the question, and I had to content myself with forming a theory based upon the known facts. Again I returned to the great Pyramid of Djoser and as I wandered in its shade and looked toward the nearby Pyramid of Userkhaf, I remembered how I had remarked jocularly to a friend, just before the opening of the sarcophagus: "Djoser and Userkhaf are talking to each other, saying that their old friend is to be reborn." Ruefully I reflected that if they were talking now they must be having a good laugh at my expense!

Yet there must be a clue to the mystery, could one but find it. My thoughts returned to the Sed Festival or jubilee associated with the Pharaoh both in his life and after his death. The main object of this feast was to renew in the person of the king the divine power which the coronation ceremonies had given him. That divine power was kingship.

I said earlier in this book that if we are to understand the meaning and purpose of Ancient Egyptian monuments we must make a serious effort to enter into the minds of the Ancient Egyptians, and this requires a considerable stretch of the imagination, particularly to those who are not Egyptologists. To those who are prepared to look at things only from the standpoint of our contemporary culture and religion, the provisional explanation I shall offer to account for the empty sarcophagus will seem farfetched and fantastic. To such I can only recommend that they read any standard work on Ancient Egyptian religion, and they will find rites and customs even more strange. To Egyptologists most of what I have to state will be familiar, although not all may be prepared to accept my conclusions.

As an example of the Sed Festival being closely connected with a king after his death, we have in Djoser's enclosure dummy buildings connected with this festival, which I have already described in Chapter One. They seem to have been intended for the use of the king's spirit in the after-life, suggesting that even after death he would need to renew his vitality at regular intervals, thus going through a perpetual cycle of rituals in which his vigor was reasserted and his coronation was re-enacted.

The purpose of several of the buildings within Djoser's great enclosure is still obscure. One of the strangest is the southern tomb, briefly described in Chapter One. I propose now to describe it at greater length, because it may throw light on the purpose of the sarcophagus in the newly discovered pyramid.

No one knows what purpose this tomb served, although there have been a number of suggestions. It is in the form of a deep rock-cut pit, of the same dimensions as those of the pit beneath Djoser's main monument, and is approached by a side ramp. In the bottom of the pit is a chamber of pink granite, again as in Djoser's pyramid, sealed in the same way with a granite plug which fits into a hole made in the flat roof. Immediately above this burial chamber is another room, evidently used for storing the plug before burial. There still remains, running from wall to wall of this room, the heavy timber beam across which ran the rope which was used for raising and lowering the plug.

The roof of this room supported the rubble with

which the pit was filled, and above that was erected a stone mastaba running east-west, mainly concealed within the great enclosure wall.

The peculiarity of this southern tomb is this. The granite tomb chamber measures only 5′ 3″ square, too small to have contained the body of a person of normal stature unless it was buried in a contracted position, a most unlikely possibility in a royal tomb of this period. Yet the "tomb" was definitely Djoser's. Nearby galleries east of the tomb chamber are inscribed with his name, and in one gallery are three stelai showing the king performing religious ceremonies, among them one showing him apparently performing the "ritual sprint" described in Chapter One.

All these stelai seem to be connected with the Sed Festival. In the southern stele he stands, facing, as always, south. He wears the tall crown of Upper Egypt, and a large artificial beard attached with straps. In front of the crown is the *serekh* frame with his name, Nether-er-Khet. The protective hawk hovers above him carrying the *ankh* sign, symbol of life, in its talons. In the middle stele he wears the northern crown and the same dress and weapons. In the northern stele he has again assumed the tall crown of the south but has discarded his tunic and wears only a belt. He runs or dances almost naked, carrying in his right hand the flail, symbol of Lower Egypt. The accompanying inscriptions are hard to understand, but several of the signs occur regularly in scenes of the Sed Festival.

Similar scenes occur in the decorated chambers beneath the pyramid itself.

J. E. Quibell, writing of this strange southern tomb, says:

> That this chamber was ever intended to receive a dead body is hard to believe. It would be just possible to get one in through the hole in the roof, but it would not be possible to lay it down at full length: the room is too small. . . . What could there have been so precious to Djoser as to merit this most expensive tomb, yet not wanted in the pyramid? His placenta? His heart, liver, etc., the usual contents of canopic vases? *Or something yet unguessed?* [1] [My italics.]

The suggestion that this might be the tomb of the royal placenta is interesting. The king's placenta had always been associated, in the minds of the Ancient Egyptians, with his ka. In his remarkable work, *Kingship and The Gods,*[2] H. Frankfort says:

"The Ka of The King is the only Ka ever shown on the monuments. It is born with the king as his twin; it accompanies him through life as a protective genius; it acts as his twin and as his protector in death. It retains the character of vital force. . . . But it is personified in a manner never observed with common people. . . . It seems that each Pharaoh was considered a twin; his

---

[1] C. M. Firth and J. E. Quibell, *The Step Pyramid*, 1933, p. 57.
[2] H. Frankfort. The University of Chicago Press, Chicago, 1948, pp. 69–70.

'brother,' however, was stillborn and passed immediately on into the Beyond, for it was the placenta, the afterbirth."

The custom of burying the royal placenta persisted until recently in Uganda, and the suggestion that it may have been observed in Ancient Egypt was made by C. G. Seligman and M. A. Murray in their paper in *Man* (1911). There is, however, no documentary evidence to support it.

Quibell goes on to say:

> We have clear evidence that the pyramid was unfinished when Djoser died, while the south tomb was closed, its stair carefully blocked and the superstructure built and cased.

Another solution to this problem is that the southern tomb was a dummy, designed for the symbolic burial of the king during the Sed ceremonies. In brief, *it was never intended to contain a body*, but was a repository for the king's ka, or spirit. Since it is fairly certain that the dummy buildings in the Sed court were not intended for use in this life but after death, there is nothing illogical in this suggestion. Examples of such "ritual tombs" are known. In the Theban Necropolis there is the "cenotaph" of Neb-hepet-Re Mentuhetep in the court of his pyramid temple at Deir-el-Bahari. Here, a sealed but empty wooden sarcophagus was found by Howard Carter in 1900, together with a statue of that king which represents him wearing the Sed dress. The real tomb lies farther west beneath the cliff.

Although it is too early to form definite conclusions,

The Mystery of the Sarcophagus

I feel fairly certain that the chamber I have discovered beneath the new pyramid is another example of a "dummy tomb" or ritual burial. No other explanation will fit the facts, and unless other evidence is produced to contradict it, I shall continue to accept it. If this hypothesis is correct, it would explain why other kings of this remote period— for example, Snofru—built two tombs.

It might also explain the existence, in several pyramids, of more than one chamber. The Great Pyramid of Cheops, for instance, has three. Besides the unfinished underground chamber, there is the so-called "Queen's Chamber" as well as the "King's Chamber." It has long been known that the former is a misnomer, as the queens were not buried within their husbands' monuments, but in smaller pyramids built outside them. If one chamber was intended for the royal body and the other for the king's ka, the presence of the two rooms would be explained. The underground chamber was left unfinished because of a change of plan by the architect. There are other examples of pyramids which were planned from the first to have two chambers. Why?

Two important questions remain to be answered. First, why was King Sekhem-Khet not buried beneath his pyramid, whereas his predecessor Djoser seems almost certainly to have been interred in the granite burial chamber beneath his monument? Second, since Sekhem-Khet was not found beneath his pyramid, where was he buried?

I shall try to suggest possible answers to these questions in the final chapter.

TWELVE

Another Mystery

BEFORE SUMMING UP THE EVIDENCE SO FAR AVAILABLE, I would like to refer the reader to another remarkable discovery made thirty years ago by Dr. G. A. Reisner near the Great Pyramid at Giza, a discovery which also revealed an empty sarcophagus, though every indication suggested that it contained a body. Egyptologists will be familiar with this story, but for the benefit of the general reader I think it should be retold.

Dr. Reisner was an American archaeologist who, in 1924, was directing the Harvard Boston Expedition when it was excavating the area surrounding the Great Pyramid of Cheops. The expedition had begun its work in 1902, and in 1924 its concession included two thirds of the great cemetery west of the Pyramid of Cheops, the area of the Pyramid of Mycerinus, and that east of the Cheops pyramid as far south as the Sphinx.

On November 1, 1924, Reisner's staff commenced work on the southwestern corner of the cemetery. It was a laborious task, first clearing away the sand, stone and rubbish down to the first-floor level, then through this to a deeper floor, and finally down to the rock itself. Every square yard of the site had to be cleared in this way, and the rubbish carefully sifted. During the process of clearing, the excavators noticed the edge of a rock cutting which ran beneath the masons' debris.

On December 12, 1924, this cutting was fully exposed and found to be the beginning of an unfinished pyramid. North of the pyramid the rock rose in a low ridge, and about 52 feet away lay the eastward edge of a quarry used for cutting stone during the reign of Cheops. In the western part the rotten surface rock had been dressed away to a depth of 12 to 18 inches in preparation for removing large blocks of stone, but the quarrying had stopped at this point.

At the end of January, 1925, Reisner returned to America to resume his duties at Harvard University. And it was on a February morning, when the Doctor was four thousand miles away, that one of his staff at Giza, an Egyptian photographer named Abdu, tried to set up his camera tripod on the masons' debris, just north of the main street of mastaba tombs, under the shadow of the Great Pyramid.

He was annoyed to find that he could not get his tripod to stick. It kept sliding on the hard rock. Then he changed his position, and found to his surprise that the tripod leg sank into what appeared to be plaster. He called Mr. Alan Rowe, a member of the expedition, and together they examined the surface. They found a patch of white plaster covering a rectangular cutting in the rock, which seemed to lead to a doorway in the south. The cutting was packed with small dressed blocks of Tura limestone set in white plaster. Soon they recognized that they had discovered an intact tomb of some sort. Course by course the packing stones were removed until, on February twenty-third, a stairway of twelve steps was revealed, which passed at the southern end of the quarry to a short rock-cut tunnel and penetrated the northern wall of a vertical shaft.

They searched for the top of this shaft, and found that it, too, had been cunningly concealed. It was blocked with stones which had been left rough deliberately so that they would look like the natural surface of the rock. It had every indication of being a secret burial.

Throughout February and March, 1925, the clearing of the shaft went on. At first the excavators thought it would be just like all the other burial shafts under mastaba tombs, that is, between 20 and 30 feet deep. At this depth they found a big slab of stone let into the west wall of the shaft, which at first they thought must lead to the burial chamber. But it did not. It simply concealed a niche containing the remains of a sacrifice: the skull and three legs of an ox. But below this the shaft still went on down, and day after day the chief workman, Mahmud Ahmed Said, and his men worked on under the fierce sun, pulling out the stones which filled the shaft and sending them up to the surface in a basket hoist.

Forty feet . . . 50 . . . 60 . . . 70 feet, and still the shaft went on down into the rock. At last, at 85 feet, one of the workmen pulled out a stone and saw a chamber beyond. A mirror was brought to reflect the sunlight down from the top of the shaft, and there the excited discoverers saw remains of gold-encased poles, golden objects, vases of alabaster, and a beautiful alabaster sarcophagus. On top of this were strips of gold, on which could be read the name of Snofru, the last king of the Fourth Dynasty and the father of Cheops himself.

When they began to clear the chamber the archaeologists found that the gold-encased poles were part of a portable canopy for the bed and other furniture of the tomb's owner. The furniture was in a fragmentary condition. The wood had decayed, and the gold leaf which had once covered it lay on the floor in thousands of tiny pieces. Yet, piece by piece, the archaeologists were able, with infinite patience, to reconstruct the sumptuous funerary furniture. It consisted of a magnificent bed, bearing the name of Snofru, two gold-covered armchairs, a gold inlaid box which had probably contained bed curtains, and a wooden box, also cased in gold, containing eight beautiful alabaster jars, each inscribed with the name of the oil or cosmetic it had held, for example: "festival perfume," "green eye-paint," and "prime Libyan oil." There was also a set of anklets of silver inlaid with a pattern of butterflies in lapis lazuli. It was clear that the tomb had belonged to a woman, but who was she? Eventually a hieroglyphic inscription was pieced together which read:

Mother of the King of Upper and Lower Egypt, follower of Horus, guide to the ruler . . . Hetephras.

The tomb belonged to Queen Hetephras, wife of Snofru, and mother of Cheops himself. The bed bearing Snofru's name may have been the king's present to his wife. These were the earliest examples found up to that date (1925) of funerary furniture and jewelry dating from the Fourth Dynasty. (The recently discovered bracelets found in the new pyramid are of the Third Dynasty, even earlier.)

But some features of the burial puzzled Reisner and his staff, and they still remain a puzzle. For example, the workmen who made the chamber had left their tools behind. Reisner wrote:

> Along the west wall lay an alabaster bowl and a heavy copper punch in perfect condition; near the middle of the bed, a massive copper instrument, perhaps a crusher, and just west of the crusher, a copper knife-blade with a riveted wooden handle. The crusher and the punch were heavy, practical, stone-cutting implements, and quite inexplicable as the funerary equipment of a queen.

Again, the poles for the support of the canopy had been laid carelessly across the sarcophagus. It would have been impossible to erect the canopy in the confined space of the small chamber. Also, mixed up with the boxes and furniture was much debris and plaster which did not seem to have come from the chamber in which the objects were found. In one box was found a flake of alabaster which had evidently been broken off the sarcophagus. They found the place from which it had been chipped.

Yet the sarcophagus appeared to be intact, and it

seemed to Reisner inconceivable that it should not contain the body of the queen. The tomb had not been robbed; the masonry filling in the deep shaft had not been disturbed, and there was no other entrance.

On March 3, 1927, in the presence of eight witnesses, final preparations were made for opening the sarcophagus. Describing the opening, Reisner wrote:

> Mr. Wheeler, directing the operations, took his place at the northern lifting jack, and Mr. Dunham with our Egyptian foreman, Mahmud Ahmed Said, at the two southern jacks. Every eye was fixed on the sarcophagus. The lid started from its place . . . and came slowly up an inch at a time. We saw the inside walls of the sarcophagus coming into view, and moment by moment looked deeper into the interior. It was soon evident that there was no inner case and finally, after ten minutes, we all realized that the sarcophagus was empty. . . .

Thus my own experience in the sarcophagus chamber of Sekhem-Khet was anticipated by Dr. Reisner twenty-seven years earlier.

There were, however, certain differences. The tomb of Hetephras contained the funerary furniture and equipment of the queen; also Reisner found, in a sealed niche opening off the chamber, the canopic jars containing the viscera which had been removed during embalmment. Therefore it would seem that in this case it was intended to place the body of the queen in the sarcophagus, but that for some reason it was removed.

Yet it could hardly have been removed from the sarcophagus while it lay in the chamber. And from the fact that the walls were rough and unfinished and that the contents were hastily packed into a room barely big enough to contain them, Reisner concluded that this was a *reburial*, and that the queen had been buried originally in another, larger sepulcher, probably near her husband's pyramid at Dashur. The evident signs of haste—the chamber unfinished, the workmens' tools left behind, etc.—suggested that the job had been done in a hurry. Why? Reisner's theory, in brief, was this. Shortly after the mother of Cheops was buried near her husband's pyramid, robbers entered the tomb and took away the body for the sake of the golden objects with which it was adorned. Probably they would have taken the furniture, too, but they may have been disturbed. Then someone had to tell the king that his mother's spulcher had been robbed, but they were afraid to inform him that the body of the queen had disappeared. Then, suggested Reisner, the king, who was then building his Great Pyramid at Giza, gave orders for his mother's body, with her funerary equipment, to be brought to Giza and reburied in a carefully concealed burial cache near his own pyramid. The workmen began their task, but when they reached a depth of 30 feet, the depth at which normally they would have made the burial chamber, they struck a patch of soft rock and had to go deeper. They went on down, making the shaft narrower, but it was not until they reached the extraordinary depth of 85 feet that they were able to find rock from which the chamber could be hewn.

Meanwhile time was getting short, and the officials responsible must have been terrified lest the secret should leak out or that Cheops should wish to see his mother's body. New orders were given to cease further work and seal up the gaps in the wall. The workmen swept the accumulated rubbish into the pit. The empty sarcophagus was lowered down the shaft, the lid replaced and covered with the rods of the dismantled canopy. The rest of the room was piled up with the remainder of the queen's furniture, mixed with debris and plaster brought from the original tomb.

Then they began to refill the shaft with stones. They were in such a hurry that they even left their tools behind. Finally, near the top of the shaft they cut a niche in the wall, sacrificed an ox for the benefit of the queen's ka, and buried the remains in the niche. While this was going on a couple of fragments of basalt from the temple of Cheops fell into the shaft and were buried in the niche —thus proving to Reisner that when the shaft was made the temple was in existence or being built. Finally, they concealed the entrance with rough stones to look like the natural face of the rock and the job was done.

This ingenious and fascinating theory was developed by Reisner purely from the archaeological evidence he found in the cache. There is no documentary evidence to support it, and the original burial place of Hetephras, if it exists, has never been found. On the face of it, it seems the most plausible explanation, and most archaeologists accept it.

Yet in view of the discovery of yet another empty sarcophagus which had not been robbed, I think the theory should be carefully reconsidered. Is it certain that the sarcophagus of Hetephras was ever intended to contain a body? The presence of the canopic jars containing her internal organs suggest that it was. Yet the interior of the alabaster box was quite clean and without stains, as was the sarcophagus which we hoped would contain the body of King Sekhem-Khet.

Perhaps this was not a reburial; perhaps from the first it was intended to bury the queen near Cheops' pyramid. But if so, why was the sarcophagus empty? Some authorities have suggested that the body may have been stolen from the embalmers' workshops, and this is a possibility. On the other hand, why, if this was the original burial, was it completed in such haste, and the queen's equipment crammed into a chamber hardly big enough to contain it?

Or was it, after all, another example of a "dummy burial," never intended to contain the actual body of the queen? It is an absorbing puzzle.[1]

---

[1] Those who wish to study this question should read Dr. Reisner's own account in the *Bulletin of the Museum of Fine Arts*, Vols. XXV (Special Supplement), XXVI, and XXX, Boston, 1927–32.

THIRTEEN

Provisional Conclusions:
The Next Stage

MORE THAN A YEAR SEPARATES ME FROM THE LAST WORDS
of the preceding chapter. Then it was June, 1954. Now
it is nearing the end of 1955, and a whole new season
of excavation lies behind me. In October, 1954, I went
to the United States of America on a lecture tour and
it was not until November that I returned to Sakkara and
recommenced my excavations. During that time I had
ample opportunity to think about the Pyramid of Sekhem-
Khet and talk to my fellow Egyptologists in America who
gave me encouragement and hope.

When I returned to Sakkara in 1954, I began my work
with new energy. The journalists, the radio and the television men had gone. The publicity which had attended
the discovery of the sarcophagus chamber had died away
and there were only my faithful workmen Hofni Ibrahim
and his brother Hussein to welcome me back, full, of
course, of new theories, and eager for me to recommence
my attacks on this mysterious monument.

I have mentioned that the entrance to the pyramid lay

at the southern end of an enormous rectangular pit cut out of the living rock on the northern side of the pyramid. This entrance led to a sloping corridor which plunged into the rock and terminated in an unfinished chamber at the center of the pyramid, some 100 feet beneath the surface of the desert. But one feature of this "approach pit" puzzled me considerably. The pit itself was cleanly cut out of the rock, but when we found the sealed entrance (see illustration 16), we had not reached the bottom of the pit. Of this I was sure, because the ground under my feet was not solid rock, but rubble. The shaft went on down below the level of the entrance which I had discovered and both Hofni and Hussein urged me to go lower, convinced that the entrance to the real burial chamber lay below.

One hundred and fifty or so workmen labored for over a month with pickaxes and baskets removing the rubble filling of the pit. At a depth of 39′ 5″ below the rock level, we hit upon another doorway which opened into the southern wall of the tunnel and led to a lower corridor, only 30 feet long, the cutting of which was never completed, undoubtedly because of the bad condition of the rock (see illustrations 14 and 16). Here we have probably the vestiges of a first attempt to cut the substructure of the pyramid. This was given up and the slope of the outer approach tunnel was reduced so that it might hit the harder layer of rock. Then, as the cutting of the upper gallery had to be carried out far down through the layers of bad rock in order to reach the sepulchral chamber, precautions were taken to cut the roof of the gallery in the form of a semicircular arch in order to give it the maximum of resistance.

Having ascertained this, we had to construct a wooden footbridge in order to regain access to the upper entrance gallery, and it was not until March, 1955, that we could carry on the exploration of the main corridor of the pyramid. The most urgent need was to complete the excavation of the last 130 feet of this corridor, lying between the shaft and the sepulchral chamber.

The season before we had passed above an enormous mass of debris which covered the floor of the corridor and might have concealed many objects. And, indeed, as soon as the first few yards of debris were removed, a large number of stone vessels were found on the floor. Hundreds of beautifully shaped bowls, dishes, plates, small tables and cups made of alabaster, schist, diorite, breccia, and porphyritic rocks, some intact and some fragmentary, lay in the passage. No food or other commodity had been placed in these vessels and most of them were evidently made for funerary purposes only. Among the stone vessels, some pottery jars with clay sealings bearing the name of Sekhem-Khet were found, thus positively confirming the attribution of the pyramid to this king. Also, the sifting of the debris enabled us to recover small golden beads and gold bar spacers belonging to one broad bracelet. This completed the collection of jewelry which was found nearby during the last season (see illustration 22b).

But the heaps of falling rock and debris rose to an

alarming height which gradually increased as the gallery widened. It was in such cases that consolidation work, to a great extent, had to be undertaken. As the rock was in a perilous condition, simple wooden supports were insufficient, and we had to build stone buttresses. And the deeper the gallery sank the higher those strengthening walls had to be raised. Toward the middle, the height of the gallery, in its present condition, attained more than 32′ 10″.

Systematic excavation enabled us to recover more stone vessels, some of which bore cursive inscriptions traced in ink. One of these gave the name of a certain Ii-n-Khnum, an official who is already known to have served under King Djoser. His name was mentioned in connection with the Sed Festival of King Sekhem-Khet. A very beautiful ivory plaque was also found. This contains a list of linens and is inscribed with the name Djeserty Ankh or Nebti-Djeserty-Ankh. Was this the *nebti* name of the king himself who would thus be the second Djoser of the Lists of Kings, or was it the name of his queen or simply that of a princess? It is still premature to decide.

Further work in the corridor resulted in the discovery of a collection of copper implements including knives, piercers, chisels and axe heads. There were also copper plates and fragments of copper vessels. A large flint knife was found near these objects.

The T-shaped complex of storerooms, which was found last season, proved to be much larger than we had thought. It was found to contain 132 storage chambers, more than the 120 we had found at first (see Chapter

Eight). The horizontal arm of the T, as we have seen, is about 495 feet long and five feet wide. Two more galleries, each about 347 feet long and running north-south, were found to branch from that gallery, at both ends of it. The compartments were cut in both sides of each of those three galleries. The whole complex seems never to have been finished. The debris of the original excavations was found to fill up the galleries and most of the compartments to about two thirds of their height.

The northeast and southwest angles of the pyramid structure were cleared. In the mortuary temple more walls appeared. These are massive walls constructed in the same manner as the pyramid structure, that is to say, with inclined courses. Some parts of the temple still retain their original pavement. But the general plan of the temple is still indefinite.

The name Imhotep appeared on one of the bastions of the enclosure wall (the White Wall). It was traced in red ink, but whether it belongs to the famous architect of Djoser is not certain. However, we have now ample reason to believe that Sekhem-Khet was Djoser's immediate successor.

One fact is certain. We are only at the beginning of the work. We have merely begun to scratch the surface. The monument itself in total area is about the size of two football fields placed side by side. The outer enclosure is over one third of a mile in length. All this has yet to be excavated. At present most of this colossal edifice lies buried under the sand, and under any part of it we may find subterranean galleries like those discovered under the Step Pyramid, any one of which may lead us to burial chambers either of the king himself or those of members of the royal family. It may need another twenty years fully to explore this monument built nearly fifty centuries ago, when almost none of the events of recorded history had yet occurred.

CHRONOLOGICAL TABLE OF EGYPTIAN DYNASTIES

Prehistoric Period
Before 4000 B.C.: settlements in various sites of Upper and Lower Egypt

Pre-dynastic Period: 4000–3200 B.C.
Transition from stone age to the use of hardened copper

Archaic Period
Dynasty I: 3200–2980 B.C.
Dynasty II: 2980–2780 B.C.

Old Kingdom (the Pyramid Age)
Dynasty III: 2780–2680 B.C.
Dynasty IV: 2680–2565 B.C.
Dynasty V: 2565–2420 B.C.
Dynasty VI: 2420–2258 B.C.

First Intermediate Period
Dynasty VII: 2258 B.C. (Interregnum)
Dynasty VIII: 2258–2232 B.C.

Dynasty IX: 2232–2180 B.C.
Dynasty X: 2180–2052 B. C.
} Contemporary with Dynasties IX–X: Intefs, Princes of Thebes: 2232–2134 B.C.

Middle Kingdom
  Dynasty XI: 2134–1191 B.C.
  Dynasty XII: 1191–1786 B.C.

Second Intermediate Period
  Dynasties XIII–XIV: 1786–1680 B.C.
  Dynasties XV–XVI (Hyksos Period): 1720–1570 B.C.
  (Local rulers at Thebes)
  Dynasty XVII: 1600–1570 B.C.

New Kingdom
  Dynasty XVIII: 1570–1349 B.C.
  Dynasty XIX: 1349–1197 B.C.
  Dynasty XX: 1197–1085 B.C.

Late Dynastic Period
  Dynasty XXI: 1085–950 B.C.
  Dynasty XXII: 950–730 B.C.
  Dynasty XXIII: 817–730 B.C. (partly contemporaneous with Dynasty XXII)
  Dynasty XXIV: 730–715 B.C.
  Dynasty XXV: 751–656 B.C. (partly contemporaneous with Dynasties XXIII–XXIV)
  Assyrian Domination: 671–663 B.C.
  Dynasty XXVI (Saite Period): 663–525 B.C.
  Dynasty XXVII (First Persian Domination): 525–404 B.C.
  Dynasty XXVIII: 404–398 B.C.
  Dynasty XXIX: 398–378 B.C.
  Dynasty XXX: 378–341 B.C.
  Dynasty XXXI (Second Persian Domination): 341–332 B.C.
  Conquest of Egypt by Alexander the Great: 332 B.C.

Chronological Table of Egyptian Dynasties

Greco-Roman Period

    Alexander the Great and the Ptolemies: 332–301 B.C.

    Roman Period: 30 B.C.–A.D. 324

    Byzantine or Coptic Period: A.D. 324–640

    Arab Conquest of Egypt: A.D. 640

BIBLIOGRAPHY

BARSANTI, A.: "Fouilles de Zaouiét el-Aryan (1904–6)," in *Annales du Service des Antiquités,* Vol. VIII (Cairo, 1907), pp. 201–10.

BARSANTI, A.: "Ouverture de la Pyramide de Zaouiét el-Aryan," in *Annales du Service des Antiquités,* Vol. II (Cairo, 1901), pp. 92–4.

BLACKMAN, A. M.: "The Rite of Opening the Mouth in Ancient Egypt and Babylonia," in *Journal of Egyptian Archaeology,* Vol. X (London, 1924).

BREASTED, J. H.: *The Development of Religion and Thought in Ancient Egypt* (1923).

BRUNTON, G.: Lahun I, *The Treasure* (London, 1920).

CARTER, H.: *The Tomb of Tut-ankh-amen* (London), Vols. I–II (1923), Vol. III (1933).

CLARKE, S., and ENGELBACH, R.: *Ancient Egyptian Masonry* (Oxford, 1930).

COTTRELL, L.: *The Lost Pharaohs* (New York, 1951).

DRIOTON, E., and LAUER, J. P.: *Sakkarah, the Monuments of Zoser* (Cairo, 1939).

EDWARDS, I. E. S.: *The Pyramids of Egypt* (London, 1954).

EMERY, W. B.: *The Tomb of Hemaka* (Cairo, 1938).

EMERY, W. B.: *The Tomb of Hor-Aha* (Cairo, 1939).

ENGELBACH, R.: "Mechanical and Technical Processes,"

Bibliography

Chapter 5 of *The Legacy of Egypt* (Oxford, Clarendon Press, 1952).

ERMAN, A.: *A Handbook of Egyptian Religion* (English translation by A. S. Griffith), (London, 1907).

ERMAN, A.: *Die Religion der Ägypter* (Berlin, 1934).

ERMAN, A.: *The Literature of the Egyptians*, translated by A. M. Blackman (London, 1927).

FIRTH, C. M., QUIBELL, J. E., and LAUER, J. P.: *The Step Pyramid* (Cairo, 1935).

GARDINER, A. H.: *The Attitude of the Ancient Egyptians to Death and the Dead* (Cambridge, 1935).

GARDINER, A. H., and PEET, T. E.: *Inscriptions of Sinai* (London, 1952).

GRIFFITH, F. LL.: "The Inscriptions of the Pyramid of Medum," in W. M. F. Petrie, *Medum* (London, 1892).

GUNN, B.: Review of T. E. Peet, "The Rhind Mathematical Papyrus," in the *Journal of Egyptian Archaeology* (London, 1926), Vol. XII, pp. 123–37.

HURRY, J. B.: *Imhotep* (Oxford, 1926).

JÉQUIER, G.: *Le Mastabat Faraoun* (Cairo, 1928).

JUNKER, H.: "Giza," *Grabungen auf dem Friedhof des Alten Reiches bei den Pyramides von Giza* (Vienna, 1929–41), Vols. I–V.

LAUER, J. P.: "La Pyramide à Degrés." *L'Architecture* (Cairo, 1936). In the series, *Fouilles à Saqqara, Services des Antiquités de l'Egypte*.

LAUER, J. P.: *Le Problème des Pyramides de l'Egypte* (Paris, 1952).

LAUER, J. P.: "Etudes Complémentaires sur les Monuments du Roi Zoser à Saqqara." In the series, *Supplément aux Annales du Service des Antiquités*.

LUCAS, A.: *Ancient Egyptian Materials and Industries*, 3rd edition (London, 1947).

LYTHGOE, A. M.: "The Treasure of Lahun," in the *Bulletin of the Metropolitan Museum of Art*, December, 1919 (Part II) (New York, 1919).

MASPERO, G., and BARSANTI, A.: "Fouilles de Zaouiét el-Aryan (1904–5)" in *Annales du Service des Antiquités*, Vol. VII (Cairo, 1906), pp. 257–86.

PETRIE, W. M. F.: *A Season in Egypt*, 1887 (London, 1888).

PETRIE, W. M. F.: *The Pyramids and Temples of Gizeh* (London, 1883).

PETRIE, W. M. F.: *The Building of a Pyramid in Ancient Egypt* (London, 1930), Part II, pp. 33–9.

PETRIE, W. M. F.: *Medum* Egypt Exploration Society, (London).

QUIBELL, J. E.: *The Tomb of Hesy* (Cairo, 1935).

RAWLINSON, G.: *History of Herodotus* (Everyman's Library, edited by E. H. Blakeney), (New York, 1912).

REISNER, G. A.: *The Development of the Egyptian Tomb down to the Accession of Cheops* (Cambridge, Massachusetts, 1935).

REISNER, G. A.: "Hetep-Heres, Mother of Cheops," in the *Bulletin of the Museum of Fine Arts*, Vols. XXV (Special Supplement), XXVI, and XXX, Boston, 1927–32.

REISNER, G. A., and FISHER, C. S.: "The Work of the Harvard University Museum," in the *Bulletin of the Museum of Fine Arts*, No. 54, Boston, 1911.

RICKE, H.: Beme-kongen Zur Egyptischen Bawkunst des Alten Reiches, II.

VYSE, H., and PERRING, J. S.: *Operations carried on at the Pyramid of Gizeh*, London, 1840–2.

Bibliography

WAINWRIGHT, G. A.: *The Sky Religion in Egypt*, Cambridge, 1938.

WHEELER, N. F.: "Pyramids and their Purposes," in *Antiquity*, Vol. IX, pp. 172–85, Gloucester, 1935.

WINLOCK, H. E.: *The Treasure of El-Lahun*, New York, 1934.